SECRETS OF THE COUTURIERS

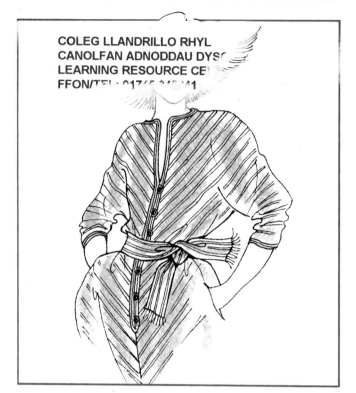

SECRETS OF THE
Couturiers
FRANCES KENNETT

ILLUSTRATIONS BY
LYNNE ROBINSON AND TERRY EVANS

ORBIS • LONDON

For my sister Catherine,
whose artistic talents and sewing skill make her
my ideal reader

ACKNOWLEDGMENTS

This book has been very much a corporate effort, much enhanced by the work of many talented people who have tried hard to understand my own tremendous enthusiasm for fashion history and design, and added their own response to the subject.

I should particularly like to thank Penny Byrde, of the Museum of Costume, Bath, who very kindly arranged for me to look at many precious items from the collection, in spite of a demanding work load. Lynne Robinson brought her flair and imagination, besides her illustrating skill, to the Designer's Notebook section; Terry Evans managed to decipher my amateurish roughs to present a beautiful collection of working diagrams; Mia Stewart-Wilson avoided all the obvious and well-known photographs to give a fresh look at the work of the couturiers; and Mary Evans, the designer, very patiently wove all these disparate elements most stylishly. To Angela Jeffs, my editor, I owe a special vote of thanks for all her encouragement and good advice; without her shaping hand the manuscript would have been a mass of notes. I should also like to thank Stephen Adamson, who had the faith in the idea to take it on in the first place – I only hope that the finished book gives everyone as much pleasure and satisfaction as it does me. And I will always remember the understanding and enthusiasm I found in Bill Gibb, whose generosity to me about my work was particularly valued as it came from someone I had admired for so many years.

Lastly, a special thank you to Thaddeus O'Sullivan, who has always listened and sympathized and enthused in such a kind way. A book is only worth writing when there are special people to share one's pride.

First published in Great Britain by Orbis Publishing Limited, London 1984

This edition published in 1985

Illustrations for 'Designer's Notebook' by Lynne Robinson
Other illustrations by Terry Evans

Phototypeset by Tradespools Ltd., Frome, Somerset
Printed in Italy
ISBN 0-85613-818-5

SECRETS OF THE

Contents

COUTURIERS

Photograph by Clive Boursnell

SECRETS OF THE

Foreword

COUTURIERS

When I was a fashion student at St Martin's School of Art and the Royal College of Art I found that books of this particular ilk were absolutely invaluable. I am proud to have been asked to write a personal introduction.

Frances Kennett's *Secrets of the Couturiers* is the product of considerable knowledge and thorough research into the inner sanctums of the couture houses and their stars. It treats us to exciting images which span from Worth in the latter half of the nineteenth century up to our distinguished contemporaries such as Valentino and St Laurent. Indeed a labour of love, *Secrets of the Couturiers* expounds the intricacies of smocking, pleating, faggoting etc., which are second nature to couturiers, but not always known by amateurs. Among the book's great values is that it elaborates in a wealth of detailed drawings how these ideas can be adapted and enjoyed by the competent dressmaker in a more simple way without losing the essence of couture.

It must be stressed how influential couture was and is in its crucial effect on the ready-to-wear for the High Street shops – this product of the rarefied world filtering into fashion stores at reasonable prices. I know, certainly, we owe much to these masters of ingenious cut and flair. It is easy to emulate but harder to instigate and Frances Kennett has successfully explained the intrinsic values of their contribution to our fashion-conscious society, making available their methods of working for the reader's benefit whether a student or a keen dressmaker who wishes to improve her skills.

I highly commend *Secrets of the Couturiers* and hope that you the reader find this most thorough work as enjoyable, informative and constructive as I did.

Bill Gibb

How to add a bow by Christian Dior, 1947.

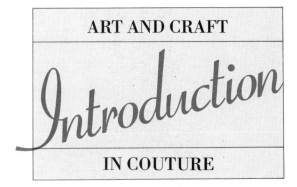

ART AND CRAFT

Introduction

IN COUTURE

This book is not just about the techniques of 'tailoring' – it is about creating beautiful clothes for yourself. There is good reason for looking at the work of the finest couturiers, in order to improve your own clothes; it is not merely in the style of decoration or the quality of workmanship that couture clothes reveal their superiority. It is that thoroughly thought-out individuality that distinguishes them from ready-to-wear. A design is only included in a collection if it can be made to look good on any individual, *without* sacrificing details or complications, which is the way that ready-to-wear clothes have to be styled. Couturiers put 'looks' together as an art, not merely a technique. That is why a good part of this book, including this introductory chapter, tries to give you some notion of the 'secret world' of the couturiers, their attitudes to women, to design, to the precise details of clothes construction, where this is relevant.

The most interesting discovery to come out of any research into couture clothes is how variable the standard of workmanship, or of finish, can be, not just from one designer to another, but from one garment to another. If you begin to think like a couturier, on a small, personal scale, your enjoyment of dressmaking will increase enormously. Saying that couture work is an art and not merely a technique is an idea that will become clear to you as you read these pages. For example, you may see a couture dress where the designer has obviously taken a step back (either from sketch or working model) and decided, in a moment of inspiration, 'What that dress needs is a bow'. And instantly there it is, a wide band of black satin, confidently stitched in place – just a plain big ribbon. Furthermore, the bow has no painstaking facing or stiffening, but is exactly what it should be – a genuine, handsome *bow*. A dressmaker's inclination would be to do the thing 'properly', and in so doing, to destroy the inherent life of the decoration. The principle secret of couture design is to suit the level of craft to the concept of the garment. Some evening dresses designed by Worth, one of the first couturiers, are positive canvases of net and chiffon,

with ribbon, bows, beads, tassels, applied in a glorious array of colour and texture – worked onto the dress in exactly the same way that a painter would give life to the surface of a canvas.

The quality that most distinguishes the work of the best designers is their immediate and total response to the feel of the fabric. Superb wool calls for fine seaming; brightly coloured taffeta demands the most subtle placing of seams to enhance the stripes, not to distort them. Chiffons must float – and the decoration on each one of these fabrics is always closely in keeping with the atmosphere that the fabric and the cut suggests. It takes students of fashion many years to learn the rules of design and styling. This book is not therefore written as a textbook – it is intended as a source book of techniques and applications, thoughts on the nature of dressmaking and the work of the couturiers, with the aim to show how a study of this field can alter the quality and the personality of your own efforts.

Of course, it is obvious that clothes today look entirely different, and serve a very different function from the ballgowns of the turn of the century, or the elaborately boned and weighted wool suits of the 'New Look' era after World War II. In the past few years, the trend has been towards loose, unstructured clothes, without stiff interfacings, or heavily tailored details. However, recent fashion collections have shown a distinct swing back towards more fitted and 'crafted' clothes. Fashions will always change, in contrast to what has just gone before; this is not mere frivolity, as some critics like to make out. How we dress reflects how we feel about living now, and must have a very current mode of expression. The desire to wear something new and different is as essential to us as changing tastes in music, film, fiction, architecture – or any other manifestation of creativity. The wonderful change in modern fashion is that it has become so much more individualized. Men and women feel free today to express their own style, create their own fashion, without slavishly following the dictates of fashion magazines or the

right *A design by Paul Poiret, 1925, combining unusual patterned fabrics boldly and with drama – a mark of the couturier's imagination and knowledge of materials. Of course a couture house has many more fabrics to choose from, but the basic principles can still be applied to the work of the dressmaker.*

opposite above *Proportion in a design is a key element in its success. The 5/8 rule works best, conforming to our conventions of balance in a design.*

below opposite *This is a beautiful example of the applied rules of proportion and symmetry. The size of pockets related to the shape of the buttons, the depth of the collar, even the spaces between the buttonholes, belt, and the set of the yoke, all precisely calculated and conveying a pleasing whole. Pierre Cardin, Autumn 1971.*

authoritative word of the great designers. The arguments about hemlines, for example, have been forgotten – almost! But while it is arguably a good aim to throw off the authority of the top designers, there is still every reason to look to them for as much information as possible about good design and good construction, so that you can be your own 'couturier'.

In one very vital area, the home dressmaker is at a great advantage. Couture clothes are distinguishable always not only by the quality of the fabric, but by the fineness of the trimming. By 'trimming' one defines all aspects of decoration of a dress, whether this includes buttons, braiding, decorative as opposed to purely functional seamlines, pockets, belts, embroidery, appliqué, and so on. The couturiers, as the following pages show, were outstandingly good at suiting the decoration to the basic fabric of the garment. That principle, already mentioned, of matching the level of craft to the concept of the garment, clearly applies here. Whereas ready-to-wear manufacturers have to pare down an exciting line, and keep trimmings within modest limits, so as not to price a garment out of the average consumer's pocket, the couturier works with little or no restriction in this way. You too can afford to decide between a run-of-the-mill belt, or special buckle, take time with hand-made buttons as opposed to plastic ones, create self-fabric trims such as rouleau, appliqué or whatever, and make your clothes truly distinctive, and individual.

In his little book, *Talking About Fashion*, Christian Dior, the fifties designer, recognizes this quality of individuality

which is so much a part of the couturier's work. (He was incidentally one of the few men in the field with an ability to express the designing process in words.)

> Everything created by human hands expresses something – above all the personality of the creator. The same thing is true with a dress. But since so many people are working on it, the real job is to get all the hands that cut, sew, try on, and embroider to express all that I have felt. In this profession, where taste is everything, I have to consider the personality of each worker at each different level. Into each hem a worker puts a bit of his or her heart and soul.

This is exactly where the home dressmaker is able to make her mark: the concept of the look should be her own, and she only has to be true to her own inspiration – and have some technical ability to execute it – to be able to create a garment that is original and personal. Why be dictated to by a magazine, even a paper pattern company, or for that matter, a book?

One area of making your own clothes that is not covered here, because it is a subject of such complexity that no justice could be done to it within the scope of these pages, is pattern *drafting*. Few home dressmakers can teach themselves pattern cutting – like so many other craft subjects, it is much better learnt with a teacher, through practice. Besides, drafting patterns really means devising new lines. Most home dressmakers are happy to work within the general outlines of current shapes and patterns – the silhouette of the moment. This book, in which nothing is beyond the skills of the average needlewoman, is based on the assumption that you will use a handful of favourite outline shapes, that suit you, and are easily adaptable. The chapters that follow will give you many ideas on how to alter or adapt those patterns, either by changing lengths, collars, cuffs, trimmings, and so on, to make your own 'custom-made' clothes.

Some principles of dress design vary very little from those employed in other forms of creative work – painting, architecture and so on. It is significant that many French couturiers, Dior, Balmain, Saint Laurent, and the Spaniard, Balenciaga, were students of architecture before going into the field of fashion. In the proportion of any design, balance above and below the waist (the natural axis point in the body) is usually maintained in a way pleasing to the eye as an artist would balance a composition. The 'Golden Mean' rule, that is a proportion of 'five parts to eight parts' that students learn about in art classes, is also a good rule of thumb for planning a dress design. While the eye accepts the natural division of the waist, a raised or dropped line cannot wander far from the five/eight division, without creating a shape that is unsettling to the eye. All distances between horizontal seamlines, and the lines of trimmings should best follow this rule: the pictures alongside illustrate this point. Pockets set on a blouse, for example, should be smaller than pockets set on the hips, to avoid a postage stamp effect created by uniform sizing. The position of bands of colour

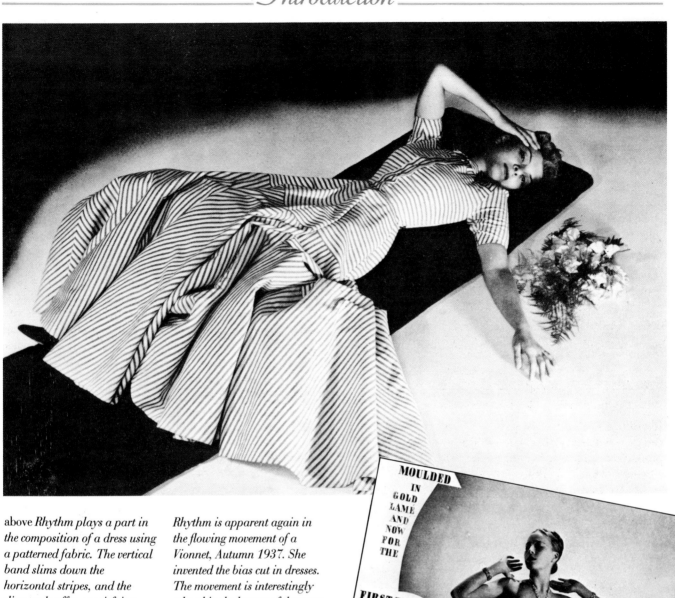

above *Rhythm plays a part in the composition of a dress using a patterned fabric. The vertical band slims down the horizontal stripes, and the diagonals offer a satisfying balance. This model is symmetrically realized, but some of the most successful dresses are asymmetrical too. Balenciaga, Summer 1938.*

Rhythm is apparent again in the flowing movement of a Vionnet, Autumn 1937. She invented the bias cut in dresses. The movement is interestingly echoed in the layout of the page from Harper's Bazaar, *Autumn 1937.*

MOULDED IN GOLD LAME AND NOW FOR THE FIRST TIME AN EMPIRE DRESS BECOMES REALLY WEARABLE FOR THE FULNESS IS STITCHED TO FALL FLAT AND SLIM OVER THE HIPS THE SILHOUETTE IS YOUNG. THE DECOLLETAGE IS TREATED MOST BEAUTIFULLY THIS IS VIONNET'S GREATEST DRESS.. A HUSH FELL WHEN IT PASSED IN THE COLLECTION..

should follow the five/eight proportion so that the shape of the garment is divided up in a balanced way. Of course, many notable designers break the rule – but they break it by playing most effectively on the existence of it in the first place. Even this is a form of 'working within the rules', not a total disregard of them. Most people sense the proportion of a design without understanding the reason why the shape is pleasing, but if you are to create your own clothes, remodelling existing patterns, then it is important to have a more conscious grasp of the basics involved.

Sometimes the concepts behind a beautifully designed dress relate more closely to music than they do to any of the other arts. This link is one that couturiers quite consciously suggest. Christian Dior wrote:

> Sometimes I have to explain the poetic mood that a dress must create. It is especially important for me to make the première understand its spirit. I really believe that beyond the meaning that comes from the work put into it, a dress must also have a soul and express it.
>
> That's why many people who are strangers to fashion can come to one of my showings and enjoy it as if it were a play. Evening dresses named after Wagner, Debussy, Richard Strauss, Henri Saugest, Poulenc and G. Auric in a subtle way remind the spectators of the composer's music.

Rhythm is one of the principle echoes of musical form that can be seen in dress. This is not quite the same thing as basic proportion – that relates to the balance between the areas of a whole shape. Rhythm is more concerned with the way details are placed on the surface of the shape – and this can include actual bands of colour in the fabric itself. Rhythm can be regular – so that buttons, pockets, strips of trimming, are placed in even relationship to each other over the surface of the cloth. Or the effect can be off-beat – so that details are placed irregularly on a perfectly-proportioned shape. Rhythm relates to the movement of the eye over the dress – does the eye travel smoothly over the detailing, or is it arrested, and made to dance about from detail to detail?

The value of 'tonal scale' is also relevant to the colouring of a garment. The illustrations give a very good idea of how the same lines of a dress can be completely altered in effect by the choice of dark shades or light tones, and the selection of contrasting colours to work with them. The first sketch is based on dark tones, with little contrast between the colours. The second is also predominantly dark in colour, but the range of tones in the colours is more striking, creating drama and movement in the dress. The third design is based on a medium-light colouring, again in a close tonal range, while the fourth sketch shows a predominantly light colouring with strong contrasts. Imagine how these different colour schemes, made in exactly the same cut of dress, could relate to women of entirely different figure types. The first design would work well for a tall, large-framed person, who needs to wear clothes that minimize her bulk rather than dividing up her shape and thus making her size more obvious. The second figure shows a fairly conventional colour scheme, easy to wear for someone with good proportions. The third would flatter someone with broader hips than bust – the classic female pear shape – because the bands of colour create a unity for the figure, while the darker shades below

Trimmings also need to be balanced well – the shape is the dominant factor in this model, but the v-shape of the bodice draws the eye up from the rounding shape of the skirt. Courrèges, 1983.

the waist would help to minimize the hips. The final sketch is perhaps the least satisfactory as the colouring tends to break up the line of the dress, but then on a large-bosomed woman, the effect could be quite attractive. In general, it is true to say that lighter colours tend to emphasize figure faults, dark colours to minimize them, and that light colours have more impact, even if used in smaller areas than dark colours.

So far, we have looked at rhythm, and proportion; the other most important element in designing which offers endless possibilities for adaptation is balance (which has inevitably been touched on in passing). Just as a face looks more beautiful when it is not quite regular – more interesting, anyway – the harmony of shape is enhanced by certain irregularity. Assuming that the form of the garment has already been decided – a favourite pattern shape that suits and fits you – then the balanced way you trim it, or shorten or lengthen the sleeves, and so on, is absolutely crucial, and makes a finished dress look like a successful new design, rather than one that has merely been re-vamped by the amateur. If you turn to the final section of this book, you will see designer details that have been 'extracted' from original designs, and offered as new ideas. But from the old to the new, the essence of the design remains, and a balance is maintained.

A design can be formally balanced – made symmetrical, with equal weight to the shapes and trimmings on both sides of the garment, as you look at the overall effect, front on. Like a pair of scales, the weight of a shape on one side, for instance a pocket, is balanced by an identical shape on the other side, at equal distance from a notional centre line. In clothing, exact balance is the normal aim because the human shape is itself asymmetrical. But designs work in a more interesting way if the elements of the composition are balanced more subtly – not with identical parts, but with disparity. Think of a child's mobile, and the idea is expressed clearly. The same applies to dress design. If you alter a collar, to make a dress look updated, then think also about the set of the pockets, the width of the sleeves, the size of the belt, the length of the dress, and the fullness of the skirt. Remember too that balance is not merely a question of trimming factors – a large pocket offset by wide sleeves. Volume and colour come into play too. Light colours have more 'weight' than dark colours. It makes a difference if the collar is white, and the pocket a dark colour, like the dress fabric. (The pockets could be much bigger in this case than if the collar were self-fabric too.) Dark colours need to be balanced by lighter colours, or the right degree of volume, or a suitable weight of trimming. The home dressmaker also has to make sure to work within the confines of the individual figure type. There is no point in devizing a dress with, for example, an arresting collar, if your neck is short, or deciding to add pockets to a bodice if your chest is very full (unless you really want to!). All this is of course a process of choice that is often familiar and unconscious, but needs practice, deliberation, and figure-analysis, as

designing for oneself involves pitfalls. Buying a dress in a shop allows you to try on and take off; once a dress is cut out, you waste a lot of time and material if the design is ill-conceived.

Balance is closely related to size and scale – as already suggested, altering one element calls for a few moments' thought about every other part of the plan. Home-made clothes so often betray themselves because they are built round a special piece of material, or a favourite object such as a lace collar or a pretty set of buttons – and it shows! A good fabric should not shriek 'look at me' – it should become you, in more senses than one.

This book will help to develop your sensitivity to scale – using the right depth of collar, the right size of buttons, tie or belt, to add emphasis. One of the delights of couture clothes is that they are very dramatic, and often very witty. There is a great difference between being dominated by a good fabric, or beautiful collar shape, and making a statement *with* it. Sometimes, dressmakers think that because they have a lovely piece of lace, for example, all it needs is a simple shape and a simple fabric to show it off. A couturier would emphasize the richness and delicacy of the piece by choosing perhaps an elaborate printed silk, or making tucks down the bodice, to echo the period feel of the lace. That is only one example of the 'thoroughly thought-out' look that is a secret of couture.

Like most other creative activities, fashion is itself an art, albeit a minor one, and it takes a great deal of looking and practice for all these elements to work well together. The following pages give you some tailoring details: classic ones, old ones that deserve reviving, and some more modern ones too. Each tailoring technique is allied to the work of one designer, so that you can see it put into practice – an end to the theorizing. And the final part of the book shows some bright new ideas, based on original designer concepts, so that you can be inspired by the process, and try it for yourself. All the ideas in the final section are based on the tailoring techniques included in this book. The possibilities for combining these elements are endless.

One last word of advice: the essence of success lies in knowing your own figure type *well*. The couturiers used to keep patterns drawn out to the exact measurements of their wealthy patrons. When they made up a model, it would be cut exactly to fit that one person. Even for a collection, each model would be made to fit one girl, and she would be selected to present that dress because it suited her temperament and her looks. Many couturiers now of course avoid this decision-making by selecting mannequins who reflect their 'look' exactly, just by nature. It may sound old-fashioned or narcissistic to say 'know your figure type'. Many women today have lost the art of presenting themselves well because some modern attitudes make them think they should not need to spend so much time looking at themselves. But every person wants to show an attractive image to the *world* – not just the *men* in it. That is part of self-expression, and very feminist!

Surprisingly, there are very few pieces of equipment used by a professional tailor that differ from the supplies of a normal dressmaker's workroom, with the exception of a few pressing items, most of which can be made cheaply and simply at home rather than purchased. Of course, the dressmaker should not skimp on some other essential items: various types of needles are to be recommended for different jobs: sharps for general sewing; betweens, which are much shorter, and make a great difference to fine hand-sewing work; milliner's needles, which are longer, for shirring, basting and hand-gathering work; and crewel needles, for decorative embroidery stitching, having a long slim eye so that several strands of thread can be used at a time. All these needles come in numerous sizes, suitable for every weight and type of fabric.

A good workbox should have several pairs of scissors – the difference these make to the finish of your work instantly repays the cost. One pair of scissors or shears should be used for cutting out very heavy fabrics, and a lighter pair reserved for cottons and finer ones. A small pointed-end pair should be reserved for clipping threads and cutting the corners of buttonholes (use only the points for buttonholes, and then there is no danger of cutting too far into the cloth). While working, you can keep the small pair tucked into a pocket, or hung on a ribbon somewhere to your side. Keep pins and needles in separate small pincushions for ease of working too. A magnet is an invaluable aid for picking up pins at the end of a complicated job. Always buy best-quality steel pins, that will not rust, and glass-headed ones for working on sheers and pile fabric.

There are so many kinds of sewing threads on the market today that the best advice is always to check, when buying any fabric, on its composition, and to match that with your choice of sewing thread. All-purpose polyesters are supposed to be useful, but some people prefer to stick to the principle of cotton thread for cottons, silk thread for silks and wools, and synthetic threads with artifically constructed fibres. Silk thread has a great deal of elasticity, and inexperienced sewers should always remember that hand-sewing has a much greater 'give' than machine-stitching – not the contrary. Hand-worked areas are less likely to split with wear than machine stitching, which can be rigid. Cheaper thin cotton is handy for light basting jobs (though it breaks easily, and is not always suitable for garments that have to be close-fitted). Button thread comes in a limited number of colours, but is much stronger than regular sewing thread: if you wish to use the same thread employed for the garment, try doubling it and rubbing it over a lump of beeswax, to strengthen and smooth the thread for button-stitching.

A few other miscellaneous items are worth remembering: a thimble is essential. It should fit so that the fingertip hardly touches inside the cap, and not constrict the top of the finger. Metal is much better than plastic, as it is thinner and stronger. Many tailors use a thimble without a head – this gives them sensitivity, but the deft sewing technique, using the side of the middle finger rather than the tip, takes some practice to acquire. Various marking methods should always be at hand in a workbox: carbon tracing paper and tracing wheel, for transferring basic lines, such as darts; tailor's chalk, in various colours, and spools of light-coloured left-over thread for making tailor's tacks. (Silk thread should be kept for basting pleats for a fine finish.) A good quality tape measure is indispensable. A skirt hem marker – a little stand with a puff ball for French chalk can be left aside – a good eye and a helpful friend are much better cultivated.

Mention will be made in succeeding chapters of the value of good pressing – quite different from ironing, which involves a forward and backward motion. For pressing, the iron is held over the area of fabric in question – usually to shrink back fullness in wool, or to flatten a particular area, such as a seam allowance. Light downward pressure is sometimes used, but often the heat and steam are sufficient to do the work. You need not own a steam iron; a plain one will do, used in conjunction with various clean cloths. You need a light muslin square (very handy for using, damp, over seams, where you want to see through the fabric as you work), a strong light cotton one for general damp use, and a thick drill piece, used dry and placed over the top of wool fabrics to prevent scorching or shine. A square of fluffy wool is handy for placing over wool fabric, under a damp press cloth of cotton, to prevent flattening of fibres – small squares of self cloth can be used for this purpose. There are also commercially available boards for pressing velvet, covered with little hairs to prevent the pile being flattened, but you can use self fabric or even terry towelling to good effect, keeping the iron slightly off the pressing cloth on top.

This emphasis on careful pressing cannot be overdone; it makes the difference between success and mediocrity in finish. Press all seams as you work – sometimes they cannot be reached properly once the garment is made up, and the effect is never the same. Shrinking through pressing helps sleeves, collars, and hems to sit very much better than otherwise, and is explained in various places in this book.

A few additional pieces of equipment will help you to work smoothly through the techniques described. A 'ham' cushion is shaped as its name suggests, and could be made easily out of old pieces of strong tweedy fabric, denim or cotton. It must be tightly stuffed with sawdust or cotton wadding, so that no wrinkles or puckers will mark a delicate fabric. A sleeve roll or seam board is a long, equally tight-stuffed shape, used for pressing seam allowances, right on the top of the curved side, so that no impression of the work is left on the front of the fabric itself. A temporary sleeve roll can be created by rolling a thick magazine up very tightly, and covering it with a double layer of smooth, firm fabric. Alternatively a wood off-cut could be used, covered with a few layers of strong padding – and made more useful if the underside is cut flat, with a curved side over the top. Sleeve boards are available, but a sleeve roll can serve this purpose just as well without extra expense: tuck it inside narrow sleeves, to flatten the underarm seam before inserting the sleeve in the armhole of a garment.

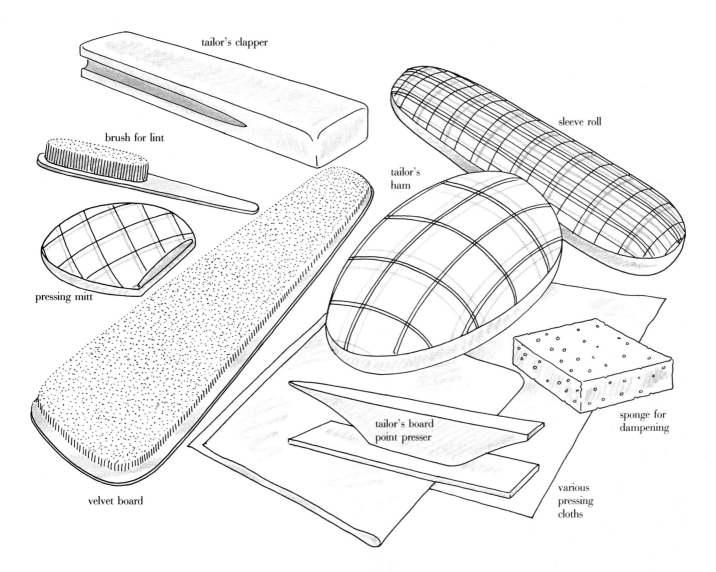

tailor's clapper

brush for lint

sleeve roll

tailor's ham

pressing mitt

tailor's board
point presser

sponge for
dampening

various
pressing
cloths

velvet board

A more elaborate piece of equipment, and one worth purchasing if you prefer classic tailored clothes, and will make much use of it, is a tailor's board – a little wooden device that has a sharp pointed end for turning out collar points and facing seams. It can be folded flat and doubles up as a 'clapper': this is a flat piece of wood, used in conjunction with much steam, to pound the seams of bulky wool fabrics to make them lie flat. It is used where excessive pressing might make the fabric shiny or matt. (A useful trick when pressing wool or gaberdine fabric seam allowances is to slip a piece of stiff card between the allowance and the fabric, to prevent a line forming. Try this for pleated skirts or dresses also.)

It is vital not to overpress any area. Just apply enough steam, either with a steam iron, or using a dry iron and damp cloth, to shrink in the fullness, or to flatten the area, as desired. Leave the fabric in place, on the board or over the shaped pad, until it has dried out and 'set' reasonably well. If you handle damp fabric, you may pull it out of shape or stretch it, counteracting the intention of pressing. To avoid

the risk of over-pressing, make sure that the cloth you use is only *damp*, not wet: a useful trick is to wet and wring out the cloth intended for use on the fabric, and then wring it again inside a towel to absorb the excess moisture.

Every garment should be pressed in this way during construction, and also once finally on completion of the sewing. Many garments should be left to hang for a day – most particularly ones with bias-cut skirts, which may 'drop' and require trimming, before the hem is pressed and stitched up. Again, allow the garment to rest and dry out completely to avoid over-stretching or distorting the shape.

When handling a new fabric, it is always a good idea to test-press a scrap of it, to see how it reacts, and to what temperature it is best suited – knowing your material is the first and most important step to successful dressmaking.

Further technical details on incorporating pressing into construction processes will be found where appropriate in the following pages. None of the techniques described there call for any other pieces of equipment other than those listed here.

House of Worth evening dress designs, illustrated in The Queen, *1892.*

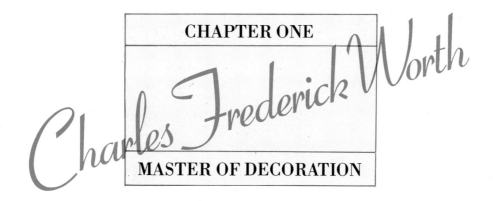

CHAPTER ONE

Charles Frederick Worth

MASTER OF DECORATION

It may seem strange that the very first couturier of any note should have been an Englishman, but Charles Frederick Worth is always considered to be the orginator of couture as we think of it today, and it is in a way quite appropriate that the first establishment in the field should have been set up in the French capital by a foreigner. Parisian fashion has always been a subject of admiration and envy all over the world – Worth understood its appeal, objectively, and had the energy and showmanship to turn style into major business.

Charles Frederick Worth was born in 1825, in Bourne, in Lincolnshire, as the son of a lawyer, who unfortunately laid ruin in his family with his passion for gambling. Although well-educated, Charles Worth was forced to enter a life of trade, and through family connections (his mother apparently coming from a slightly more middle-class background than her husband) secured an apprenticeship at the new London store of Swan and Edgar. This starting place was entirely appropriate: Swan and Edgar's was one of the very first London stores to be opened, in 1886; William Edgar and John Swan were both in their own way also pioneers, having been market stall men selling their drapery wares in provincial towns.

Worth's apprenticeship was useful because he learnt how to listen to his customers, and gained a valuable insight into the tastes of the rising bourgeoisie. And outside, in Piccadilly, he had the chance to see the wealthiest and most stylish people in London parading up and down.

Worth left London in 1845 to make his way to Paris: from his years at Swan and Edgar's he had imbibed a love and admiration for the magical French names that were so admired by his customers: Rose Bertin, the milliner; Duvelleroy, the master of fans; Guerlain and Houbigant for perfumes. He began humbly by securing work at a small but very fashionable shop, Gagelin and Opigez in the rue Richelieu. His background, selling shawls and fabrics in London, was undoubtedly helpful, as the new shop specialized in shawls, cloaks and mantles, known in those days as 'confections'. Very close by lived the court dress-maker, Leroy, who ruled the roost as far as high society fashion was concerned. His styles, exquisitely sketched in the numerous fashion plate magazines of the time, would be interpreted by dressmakers for individual clients; and these dressmakers, at the time, were all women. It is interesting, and at the same time a sad social comment, that Parisian couture had to fall into the hands of a man in order to become an industry, world-renowned.

In the 1850s Worth married the woman who was to be a great support and collaborator in his life's work: Marie Vernet, who had also been employed at Maison Gagelin. She had tremendous style, and Worth enjoyed designing dresses for her, copying some of the ideas he had seen, but just as often thinking of new shapes and trimmings to suit her. Eventually he asked the sewing department at Maison Gagelin to make some of his ideas up for Marie to wear. Soon, customers were commenting on Marie's clothes, asking her which dressmaker she used, and it was not long before some of them appealed to the managers of the store for copies of Mme Worth's dresses. At first these requests were refused, because 'couturière' work was considered inferior to trading in fine stuffs and rich mantles. But eventually, the pressure from the public ensured that Worth got his way, and he began with a small dressmaking department, producing toiles (canvas versions of his designs) from which the customers could select a model, and then choose a fabric in which they would have the dress made up.

Inevitably, Worth had to move on. Although the dress-making venture was a great success, and earned Maison Gagelin a great deal of money and reputation, Worth profited little from it directly. In 1858 he decided to give up his security and go into partnership in his own designing and dressmaking concern. His greatest piece of fortune came a few years later when his wife approached Princess Pauline de Metternich, wife of the Austrian Ambassador, and newly

above *A typical Worth design, 1892: patterns for bodices and sleeves would be kept for many years, re-used and re-styled for each season. The appliquéd lace and the high sleeve-head are characteristic of the ornate, decorated formality of Worth's designs.*

below *Three day outfits, 'Toilettes de Casino', c.1890. The decoration was often dabbed onto the surface of the fabric, as an artist would work on canvas.* left *Pin tucks, shirring, fringing, all add opulence to women's figures. They were meant to symbolize their husbands' wealth in their dress, to look like acquired works of art.*

arrived in Paris. Marie showed her some of Worth's designs, and succeeded in getting an order for a new ballgown from her. This the Princess wore to Court, at the Palace of the Tuileries, where the Empress Eugènie herself complimented her on the design of her dress, and, from that moment on, Worth's success was assured. He rapidly became established as the couturier to the *haut monde*, and rather than follow orders from his employers, Worth managed, by force of character and sheer inventiveness, to impose his own concepts and ideas on his clients. In so doing, he became the first real 'Couturier' as opposed to court dressmaker.

One of Worth's most long-lasting influences during his years at Maison Gagelin was the creation of the crinoline, although in later years he came to hate its ubiquity. The Second Empire was a time when a certain dramatic unreality had taken hold of high society; clothes became symbols of position, luxury, decoration, much more so than in previous or succeeding times. It was also a time when many newly wealthy ladies were not at all sure of themselves: a new aristocracy was in the making. Such women were relieved to turn to a man like Worth, and rely on his good judgement about their dress. As for the truly wealthy, Worth would be a hard man: he insisted on using only the very finest materials, and would often rip apart a dress that a customer was already quite delighted to have, in order to remake some part of it to a more original conception. One of the reasons why

Worth was such an expert with trimmings and decorations was the impossibility of dislodging the eternal crinoline from favour; as long as it lasted, however, Worth used all his ingenuity to decorate these extraordinary shapes in a variety of interesting ways.

It must be remembered that many of his designs were hardly clothes in the modern sense of the word: his clients might wear a delicate and frothy creation merely for a ride in a carriage, or a more or less immobile evening in a theatre box. It is not surprising therefore that the lace trimmings, tassels and bows should have been of an insubstantial and opulent nature entirely unsuited to modern dress. And besides, the volume of work his ateliers were required to turn out called for some simplification in cutting and sewing; on one occasion in 1866, for the guests of one of the '*scénes élégantes*' at the Chateau du Compiègne, Worth produced no fewer than 1000 ballgowns, each to be made within a week.

To give some idea of the value of these clothes, a letter from one of his customers describes: 'For a private fancy dress ball at the Tuileries last Monday Worth made costumes to the tune of 200,000 dollars, and yet there were not 400 ladies invited'. Given the increasing competition among new couturiers in Paris (largely generated by his own efforts) it is unlikely that Worth made more than 100 out of the 400 models, perhaps giving some idea of the luxury of his trade. But there had to be short cuts or new techniques to cope with the volume of work. As a description of his work, given in a catalogue from the Brooklyn Museum in 1962, explains:

Each pattern must have done yeoman work at the House of Worth. An oblong skirt drapery introduced in the late 1860s continues basically unchanged into the late eighties. It may be trimmed with fringes, bands or fluting, or finished with rosettes, but the pattern remains the same. The gracefully pointed edge of an 1870 skirt is used again and again in the 1880s and 1890s until it disappears under the skirt to trim a turn-of-the century petticoat ... His gowns were made of many standard interchangeable parts – one sleeve could fit a variety of bodices.

Often, Worth would make the original version of 'separates': two bodices would often be made to match one crinoline skirt: one for daytime, like a military jacket or 'chasseur' as it was called, matching the skirt and with a pointed velvet corselet, while the evening bodice, cut on different lines with long curving seams from the armhole to the waistline, was completely lined in starchy book muslin to hold and control the shape.

Another aspect of Worth's success, and one that is the basis of fine couture work, was his imaginative and entirely flexible use of fabric. He played with the innate character of a textile so that its chief attributes come out to perfection. For example, a morning dress of 1880 was made in embroidered chambray, all done by hand. Instead of darts, which would have disturbed the tiny flower pattern of the fabric, the bodice was shaped back and front alike by using shirring, and the only boning in the dress was inside the skirt, held to a round bustle by tapes. To match the delicacy of the shirring, a fluted linen ruffle covered the neckline of the bodice.

A further elegant description from the Brooklyn museum exhibition gives some idea of the fineness and luxury of the House of Worth's work, at the beginning of the century: (of a tea gown dated 1899):

Stiff taffeta brocaded in deep pink stripes and roses à la Pompadour is set against soft blue chiffon, ruched, pleated, draped and lavish with lace. The taffeta is cut like a surcoat on a princess line. Underneath is a closely fitted sheath of iridescent pink satin completely shrouded in blue chiffon. This supple fabric is more than usually mobile and clinging, since it is cut on the bias. Underneath this is a handsomely shaped foundation of white taffeta, well boned, hooked and taped.

Or what could be more beguiling than this Cinderella style ball gown, made in 1902:

A front panel is formed by cutting out the design of the fabric and appliquéing it to lace with a fine chenille cord: the whole is mounted on crisp taffeta veiled in chiffon. A misty hemline is made of the chiffon cut in double circles and edged in three rows of ruching.

It was workmanship like this that enabled Worth to make the difficult switch in tastes from the grandeur of the Second Empire to the new Republic in the 1870s. He continued to find favour with the stars of the French theatre, such as Sarah Bernhardt and Eleanora Duse, and the new influx of clients from America. During this time, his two sons, Jean and Gaston, came into the business, and they continued to work as couturiers of some note until well into the 1920s. Gaston Worth was responsible for organizing the Chambre Syndicale de la Couture Française – the organization for the couture industry that protects its members.

Charles Worth gradually retired more and more to his luxurious estate at Suresnes, on the outskirts of Paris, and died in 1895. The *London Times* published a comment on his work which serves as an inspirational reminder of the aims of the first, and probably of all truly great couturiers:

At times he had to work out 'a scheme of costume' laboriously and according to the principles he had learned by long experience and severe application. In moments of inspiration a great conception came to him like a flash ... the demands upon his judgement in form, colour and texture must have been severe. There are models whom no expenditure of time, thought, and dollars can drape successfully.

Yet no man – no woman certainly – who had seen his or her friends transfigured by Worth toilettes has ever failed to pay homage to his inimitable art in 'clothing the palpable and familiar with golden exhalations of the dawn'. The experience afforded the spectators a glimpse of a better world, if occasionally it filled their fair bosoms with some of the worst passions of this ...

Here are a few of the decorative techniques employed in the House of Worth. Although some of these may seem elaborate at first glance, they are no more complicated to achieve than patchwork, macramé, or any of the other handicrafts currently enjoying popularity. There also seems to be no good reason to separate clothing from other artefacts when it comes to decoration.

It is interesting that many of the original Worth gowns, particularly the evening wear, display a strange mixture of perfection and lack of finish. Quite often the edges of dresses made in satin or brocade are not hemmed at all, but have elaborate, heavily jewelled edging hand-basted over the raw

edge, or ribbons casually gathered and festooned down the side of an unfinished overskirt opening. Of course these gowns were carefully worn over stiff under-petticoats, on few occasions. Nowadays, by comparison, we are still used to allowing for high dry-cleaning bills for even quite simple garments made of a different fabric. So in reality, hand-crafted work presents no greater a problem of maintenance now than it did then. Worth dresses were 'costume', meant to create an impact, a statement for the wearer. In the narrowing down of options created by ready-to-wear, such detail that can be achieved by hand brings back that individual flair to dressing.

To MAKE A BOWED LACE INSET FOR A SKIRT OR DRESS PANEL Choose a reasonably lightweight and non-fraying material base, such as cotton, lightweight woven wool, crêpe, good quality brocade or satin.

Form a wide lace ribbon – 3.75cm (1½in) would be suitable – into a flat bow as shown, and pin it in position on the right side of the fabric (FIG 1).

Baste the ribbon firmly in position, with small stitches so that the edges of the lace remain straight. If you intend to make more than one lace inset,

trace the shape of this first bow so that all subsequent ones can be matched up exactly to the pattern you draw.

Stitch all round the outer edge of the lace, carefully sewing through the double layers of lace at the loops of the bow to hold it securely in place (FIG 2A, 2B). Press gently, then cut away the fabric from behind the laced area (FIG 3).

Hand-overstitch the cut edges on the wrong side of the fabric for a neater effect, taking care not to pull on the threads of the lace itself. Press lightly.

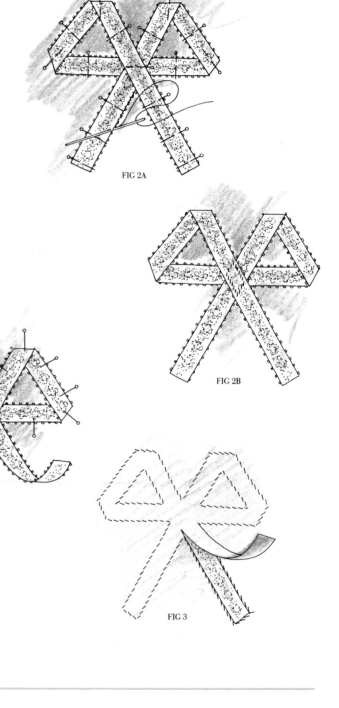

FIG 2A

FIG 2B

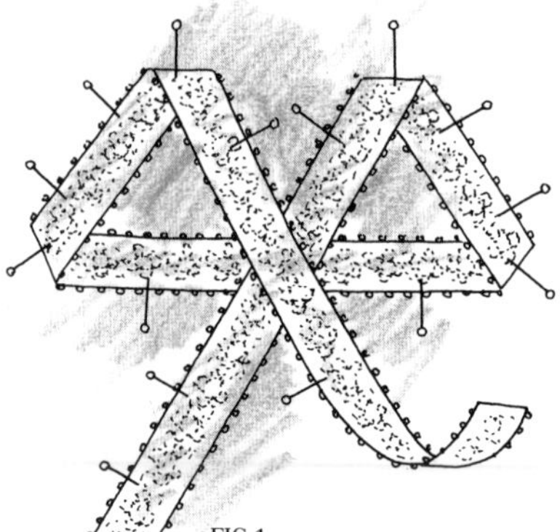

FIG 1

FIG 3

GAUGING

Gauging is an old fashioned form of gathering, similar to smocking, but producing a firm, non-elastic fabric. It was used by Worth for dresses made in fabrics that gave a design a delicate overall appearance, where he did not want to spoil the material – and so the garment – with darts. Lacy fabrics, broderie Anglaise, for example, are all suitable for this technique.

Gauging could be applied to any dress pattern where elasticated gathers are planned for the waist or neck area, or where you can adjust the darts, opening them out slightly to allow for more material to be cut into the bodice section. You will need about double the exact fitting size for the midriff to make the ruching successfully. Bell-shaped sleeves, for example, could quite easily be gauged instead of gathered into a cuff.

Run three or more parallel lines of basting across the area of fabric to be gauged. Little tubular tucks will form as you gather up the fabric. It is important to ensure the tucks are of an equal depth and also equal fullness for the best effect. Draw up the threads and secure by winding the ends round a pin head in a figure of eight motion, then space the gathers so that they are exactly even in fullness (FIG 4).

A useful trick is to hold the fabric, top and bottom, outside the area of gauging, and then to give it a quick sharp pull to straighten out the pencil gathers (FIG 5).

Measure the fabric to check that the gauging is gathered to the correct width of the bodice or sleeves or other area. For the bodice, it may be necessary to pin and tack the front and back together to check the fit and the depth of the gauging around the midriff.

Once correctly fitted, the traditional way to secure the gauging is to mount a light net backing. Working from the wrong side, baste over the gathered area, lightly attaching the net in position. Then, working on the wrong side, take small running stitches in the back part of each tuck, so that the fronts remain rounded and stand out (FIG 6).

A lightweight lawn, or woven interfacing could be used instead of net, if preferred.

An alternative, quicker version is to run a braid or *rouleau* (see page 86) across the front of the gauged lines of stitching, and then to hand-stitch the decoration in place over the top of the tucks (FIG 7).

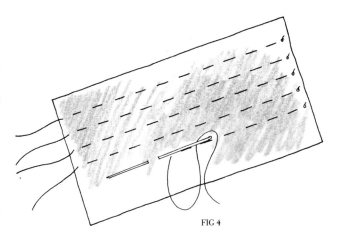

FIG 4

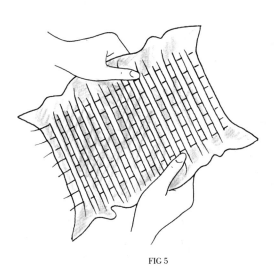

FIG 5

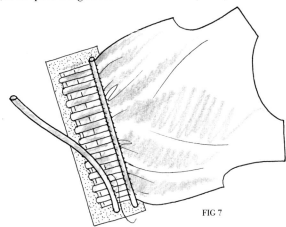

FIG 7

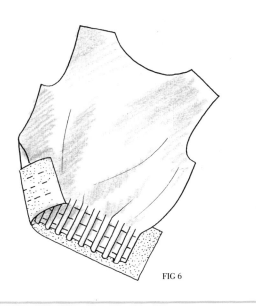

FIG 6

CORDED SHIRRING

This is a very pretty version of shirring that makes an attractive decorative finish for the area between the waist and hipline of a full skirt in place of pleats, gathers, or large darts.

Allow extra to the length of your skirt, equal to the depth of the total number of tucks, which will be about 2cm (¾in) each time. Simply baste lines where the gathered, corded effect should be placed (or mark with tailor's chalk). Fold in half and run a row of small machine stitches, keeping the foldline exactly centred on the basted or pencilled line, 9mm (⅜in) either side of the fold (i.e. half the 2cm (¾in) allowance) (FIG 8).

Using a bodkin attached to a silky piping cord, thread the cord through the tucks so formed. Gather the fabric evenly along the corded tuck, until the fullness over the hip area is completely and evenly taken up. The ends of the cording can be hand-stitched to the tucks, cut just short of the side seam stitching line (FIG 9).

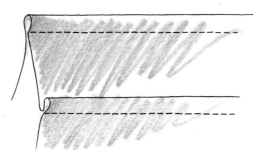

FIG 8

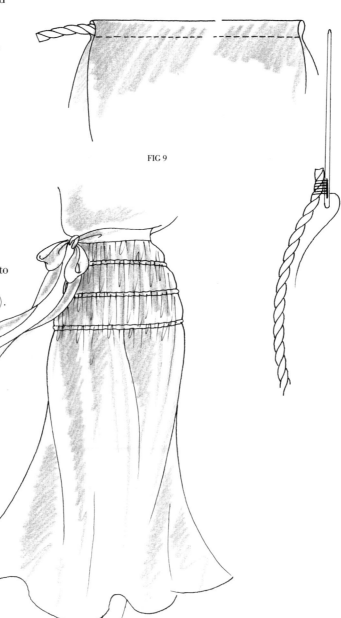

FIG 9

BIAS-FOLD, SHELL TRIMMING

This lovely edging has a particularly Edwardian look to it, although a glance through Paris fashion models from 1900 to 1960 shows that it returns periodically into favour. The process is time-consuming, but the finished effect is very special indeed. Use the edging mounted in bands, for a skirt border, or tuck a line of these trimmings into the edge of a seam for a cuff or collar, as illustrated.

Choose a lightweight fabric: coloured lawn is recommended but any cotton, firm silk or even taffeta would do. For a cuff or collar, 5cm (2in) squares are a reasonable size; for a skirt border, slightly larger, 7.5cm (3in) squares are easy to work. Cut the squares of fabric to the size preferred; fold first in half, and then into a triangle as shown (FIG 10).

Baste each one across the bottom raw edge to secure the folds. Pin, then baste the 'shells' in a straight line (marked with French chalk or basting for accuracy) across the skirt or other applied area.

If the skirt is flared, then the best method of applying the shells is to cut long bias strips of skirt fabric. Make the strips about 10–12.5cm (4–5in) in width (depending on the length of the skirt, your height etc – use your own judgement for the exact proportion). Join the strip into a circle, exactly fitting the circumference of the skirt. Fold the bias strip so that 1cm (½in) stands out on one edge of the fabric, then fold this down to cover the raw edge of the other side (FIG 11A, 11B).

Pin, then baste this folded strip over the little shells, already mounted in a row in position, covering their bottom edge by about 9mm (⅜in). Machine stitch along this line (FIG 12).

Rows of shells with bias borders look especially effective if they are spaced in progressively wider bands, round the bottom of a skirt.

A simpler, quicker method of mounting the shells would be to cut a narrow bias strip, say 5–7.5cm (2–3in) wide, join it into a circle and match it to the circumference of the skirt, as before. This time, however, merely iron or baste a single turning on each long raw edge; then pin and tack the bias trim over the mounted shells, and machine stitch along both edges, top and bottom, appliquéing the strip into place (FIG 13).

The first version would give a more authentic tuck, the second, a firmer quicker finish.

The shells can also be mounted into a collar or cuff facing: reduce the size of the shells, as already suggested. Place them pleat-side facing down on to the right side of the collar or the top section of a cuff. Try to arrange them so that you have the exact number of shells to fit along the edge, adjusting the width of the shells accordingly. Mount the facing piece over the shells once they are basted into position, and stitch in the usual way (FIG 14).

Remember to use only lightweight material so that the thickness of the shells does not present a stitching problem, or make the garment difficult to launder.

FIG 10

FIG 11A

FIG 11B

FIG 12

FIG 13

FIG 14

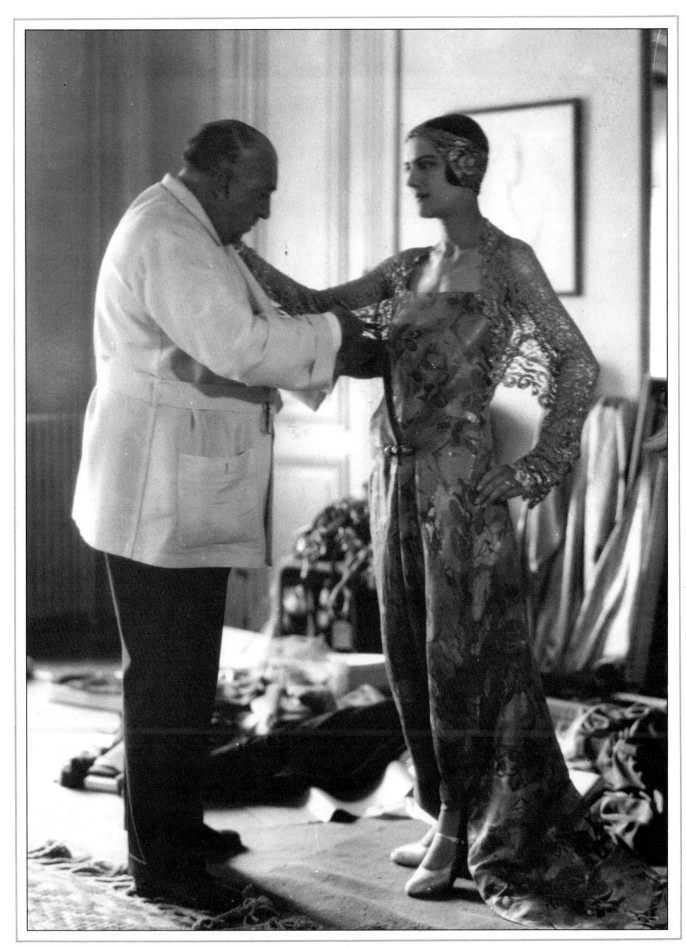

Paul Poiret at work on one of his designs, 1913.

CHAPTER TWO

Paul Poiret

ARTIST IN FABRICS

When the great Art Deco exhibition was arranged in Paris in 1925, the organizers paid this tribute to Paul Poiret, the leading couturier of the second decade of this century:

> It is possible to hold this event only because of the impetus that Paul Poiret has given to modern decorative arts by founding the Martine School and Shop and encouraging professional interior decorators.

Just a year earlier, the great Poiret had been awarded the Legion of Honour, and was addressed with these words by an equally distinguished couturier, Jacques Doucet:

> I wish to tell you how richly you deserve your decoration and acknowledge that in our profession of making women beautiful your efforts have been immense and that we owe you an incalculable debt. You have re-made fashion. From you comes the principal part of everything that now makes our country the world centre of feminine beauty and grace . . .

But Poiret was never a man to proceed through life without a fair share of criticism: in *Kings of Fashion*, Anny Latour describes his achievement less flatteringly:

> Hair and turban mounted with an *aigrette* pulled down to the eyebrows, a narrow draped dress and a loose bright-coloured kimono blouse; eyes painted with black pencil, a hand on the hip, swaying slowly and languorously in a *corte*; this was the attire of the fashionable woman – the 'vamp' type – who, dressed by the Sultan of Fashion, danced her way gaily towards the world catastrophe.

Such conflicting views can be reconciled. Poiret's achievement was at first to bring liberty to women's dress: to provide a new style sufficiently daring that it literally forced women out of their 'S' bend Edwardian corsets in the space of a year. Poiret also brought an entirely new palette of colours into fashion – no doubt influenced by other current artistic events, such as the Russian invasion of Paris, with the Ballet Russe which brought 'orientalism' to the city with such a cultural fanfare, and, later, the interest in African art suggested by the Cubists. Poiret was the first couturier to see his work very much as an *art*, not merely artifice: it is not surprising that he branched out into so many other areas of work – fabric design, furniture design, perfumery and cosmetics, accessories of all sorts. To all these activities he brought an overall 'Poiret' signature, or concept, as it would be termed today. It is an indication of how far ahead of his time Paul Poiret was that Pierre Cardin is often mentioned as the first couturier to have realized many of Poiret's aims. On the negative side, there is no doubt that he was shamelessly egocentric, and in later years, unable to adapt to changing currents in fashion.

It is almost a contradiction in terms to include Poiret in a survey of the best 'tailors' of Paris, for by his own admission he could hardly sew on a button (as a rather dismayed official discovered during the First World War, when Poiret had to report for active service to the army's 'tailoring' division). But just as Worth epitomizes the French art of decoration and adaptation at its finest, so Poiret was the first couturier to make a totally creative exercise out of the use of fabric itself. Many of his designs are structurally quite simple, but achieve their effect because of the imaginative use of material, the exotic colouring he introduced (many new dyes were created by him in collaboration with the artist Raoul Dufy, together with a chemist, hired specially to experiment with new mordants, resistants and so on). Instead of the heavy, ornate fabrics of the Edwardian era, Poiret sought out silks, brocades, soft velvets, lamés, and furs. The shapes he created were soft, supple, and called for an entirely new body beneath. Edwardian women were all bust and buttocks. Poiret's ladies were, apparently, several inches taller, lithe, much less curvaceous, but frequently, even more sexually attractive. Poiret himself, though short, plump and bearded, had considerable charm and a magnetic personality. He thought nothing of haranguing any of his clients who dared

Considering it is over 60 years old, the dash and cut of this Poiret dress and cloak design is inspiring. Abstract shapes figure in fashion fabrics for the first time, a complete contrast to the lavish work of Worth in previous years. Winter 1920.

to disagree with his decisions, and often ordered them out of his salon with a bellow. Most of his clients adored it.

The grandiose flowering of Poiret's personality seems to have taken seed early in his life: though humbly born in 1879 to parents who ran a small wool textile shop in Paris, he was a precocious child, difficult to control. His father sent him to a Jesuit school with very high academic standards, presumably in order to subdue him. Although his early education was chaotic, due to his lack of discipline, Poiret ended up with remarkable results in both sciences and arts.

In spite of this success, his fascination for the work of contemporary artists like the Fauves, and his frequent trips to the theatre often caused conflict with his father.

Again in an effort to make Poiret realize his station in life, he was denied further education and instead apprenticed to an umbrella maker, but the very limits imposed on him only added fuel to the fire. Poiret spent most of his spare time making up dresses for a little model doll, an unusual present from his sisters. At least the umbrella shop job allowed him to make deliveries to wealthy clients where he caught glimpses of fine ladies in their own setting. His talent was obvious: even as an unknown, Poiret succeeded in selling his designs to the house of Chéruit, in 1898. He also submitted sketches to Jacques Doucet, then the leading figure in couture circles, and was delighted to have them accepted. Shortly after, Doucet found an opening for a junior assistant and took Poiret on. It is a demonstration of his own taste that he gave Poiret so much freedom – even allowing him to create a few designs for some of his most distinguished customers, the actresses Réjane and Sarah Bernhardt. In fact, his first model, for Doucet, a short red wool cape, was so well received that the house received 400 orders. Poiret also began a long and equally distinguished career as theatrical costume designer with a commission to dress Sarah Bernhardt for her heroic role in Rostand's *L'Aiglon*.

It was obvious however that his personality and talent would never submit to employment by others, and eventually an embarrassing row with clients forced Doucet to fire Poiret. After a brief spell of military service, Poiret found himself, at the age of 22, in the house of Worth, now run by the great man's two sons, with Gaston as business manager and Jean as chief designer. Gaston wanted Poiret to design some 'bread and butter' models – or as he himself put it, 'fried potatoes for a restaurant that serves nothing but caviar'. An enormous disparity in taste and aims between Poiret and Jean doomed the arrangement from the start.

By the age of 24, Poiret knew that he had to strike out on his own, and his mother, who had been widowed by this time, lent him some funds. The little salon attracted great attention due to the novelty of its window-dressing, but few customers actually entered and bought, until Doucet, ever-interested in his protégé sent the magnificent Réjane to become his first patron. Soon, all the wealthy ladies in Paris were flocking, curious and eager, to see Poiret's extraordinary designs. Of his own new colours, Poiret wrote:

On the pretext that it was distinguished, all vitality had been suppressed. Nuances of nymphs' thigh, lilacs, swooning mauves, tender blue hortensias . . . all that was soft, washed out, and insipid was held in honour. I threw into this sheepcote a few rough wolves – reds, greens, violets, royal blue – that made all the rest sing aloud.

Equally revolutionary was his new shape. Taking his inspiration from the draped dresses of ancient Greece, he created simple tubes of dress that fell from the shoulders, often with a wide, bateau neckline, and decorated with a small detail, – a tassel, a belt, a buckle, that added a hint of coquetry to the simplicity of the shape. Of this new development he wrote:

While studying sculptures of ancient times, I learned to use one point of support – the shoulders, where before me it had been the waist. This new basic principle caused fashion to evolve towards classical antiquity . . . Fabrics flowed from this ideal point like water from a fountain and draped the body in a way that was entirely natural.

As was the case with the elder Worth, Poiret was greatly helped in launching his work by his wife, Denise, for whom he began to create clothes in 1905 (during their engagement). With her tall statuesque figure and dark, exotic good looks, she typified the woman he wished to dress. Throughout most of his career, she was a strong, often moderating influence on his extravagant nature, and certainly worked hard as his most publicized and photographed model.

After a while, Poiret developed the original slim tunic idea by adding a second, or even third shorter layer over the top: the basic *fourreau* or sheath would be made out of a single length of fabric. By the end of the first decade, 1910–11, a fuller 'sack' shaped dress came into vogue.

His biographer, Palmer White, whose sympathetic portrait of Poiret describes a character of tremendous energy and talent, quotes his philosophy of design in *Vogue*, 15 October, 1913:

To dress a woman is not to cover her with ornaments; it is to underscore the endowments of her body, to bring them out and stress them. It is to reveal nature in a significant contour which accentuates grace.

Paris society was frequently shocked by these first displays of 'contour'. When he took his mannequins to the Longchamps racecourse in 1909 wearing Hellenic dresses, slit to the knee, respectable doyennes led their gaping-mouthed husbands swiftly from the scene. Poiret had caused the first of many scandals. But eventually he won the day – so much so, that a few years later, in 1910, he was able to introduce hobble skirts, practically preventing his ladies from walking. And then all Paris wore them. As Poiret wrote, irrepressibly:

Yes, I freed the bust, but I shackled the legs! Women complained of being no longer able to walk, nor get into a carriage. Have their complaints or grumblings ever arrested the movement of fashion, or have they not rather, on the contrary, helped it by advertizing it? I made everyone wear a tight skirt.

Although his braggadoccio seems not entirely attractive, Poiret can be forgiven, on account of the long list of innovations that justified his rather inflated view of himself. He introduced turbans and various delightful head-wrapping ideas, to complement the simplicity of his long robes. He created the fashion for the kimono coat, as early as 1906 – a shape that has gone on playing a significant part in fashion right up to the present day. He was the first (in a delightful book, a self-publicizing volume launched in 1911–12 entitled *Les Choses de Paul Poiret*, by the artist Georges Lepape) to design various pantaloon shapes, veritable 'boiler suits'. He also launched the fashion for boots worn with straight, side-slit dresses – morocco, laced-up versions, which look as pretty now as when his wife Denise shocked the citizens of Paris with them in 1908.

Poiret was first in many, many other ways. He was the first couturier to tour with mannequins to sell 'export' models of his clothes, to Russia in 1911, and to the USA in

1920: Hemlines began to rise, and shapes became looser, easier to wear, but still lavishly trimmed. Many of Poiret's designs show strong ethnic influences, like these Russian ensembles, and can still suggest amusing ideas for modern clothes.

1913. Poiret wanted to sell his designs there under licence; but was incensed to discover that after the initial outrage at his new look, all his dresses were busily being pirated. It was only when the later couturiers of the second 'New Look' actually sued at law (Dior in particular) that model dresses were protected by copyright laws. Poiret was also the very first couturier to think of launching his own perfumes and cosmetics in 1913. Characteristically, he designed everything, the bottles, the packaging, entirely himself. Another project, which to this day stands as an outstanding example of artistic dedication, was his creation of a school for girls from limited backgrounds, where they were paid an income, given regular meals, and, after a short period of formal training were left to their own devices to create design ideas. The 'Martines' as they were called, were named after his second daughter (the first, Rosine, lending her name to the perfume factory and its output). The girls were sent to factories to see cloth being woven, to the atelier where Dufy worked on dyeing and printing on the couturier's fabrics, anywhere where Poiret thought they might find educative inspiration. The girls variously created rugs, ceramics, textiles, furniture ideas, and were paid a bonus on the designs that went into production. Proof of the remarkable success of this venture came in 1912, only a year after the school was opened, when the girls commanded two rooms for a display of their work at the Autumn Salon des Arts Décoratifs.

Aside from his many work interests, Poiret captivated the *beau monde* of Paris with his lavish parties and other entertainments. Some were Arabian nights fantasies, where everyone attended in fancy dress. The costumes were so fascinating that they themselves were turned into fashion – notably the 'Sorbet'-inspired designs, taken from the dress he made for Denise to wear at the 'Persian Celebration' he gave in 1911 for 300 guests. The dress had a hooped overtunic, christened the 'lampshade', and tight pantaloons beneath, all made up in shimmering chiffons and cloth of gold with gold fringe to the skirt, and fur trimming to the sleeves.

Eventually however, the brightness of his reign dimmed. When he returned from a frustrating period of military service during the First World War, where his talents were singularly under-used, he found himself faced with mounting debts from his inactivity during the war years. He plunged from one extreme scheme to the next, finally in 1924 allowing his couture house to fall into the hands of unsympathetic financial directors, who never co-operated with him (not an easy task for even faithful supporters at any time). He dwindled through his remaining years, spending any money that came his way with unrepentant profligacy. His post-war collections never regained the supremacy that he had enjoyed before: in 1923 the leading fashion magazines did not even bother to cover them. Occasional honours came his way, but his house finally closed in 1929. Only the generosity of friends maintained him in his final years, and there were even periods when he lived in extreme poverty or on the dole. He died in 1944, somewhat

Mme Poiret, Denise, his favourite model and inspiration, wearing one of the 'Grecian' robes, 1911, in a romantic print – showing the eclectic tastes of Poiret. Soon the underskirt would be abandoned.

comforted in his final months of impoverishment and illness by an exhibition of his paintings, arranged through the kindly efforts of André Villeboeuf, a painter and writer, which re-united him with many of his former friends and acquaintances.

It is often thought that great couturiers would have preferred to rise to success in other careers; architecture is often bandied about as the chosen métier. Paul Poiret, though an endlessly creative person, was always an artist – with clothes. His extravagant life, with victories and reversals, was a fragile affair. Fashion is always changing, ephemeral by nature; so was Poiret's spirit.

One of the changes brought into fashion by the designs of Paul Poiret was his masterly handling of boldly patterned fabric. It is one aspect of couture work that ready-to-wear finds hard to emulate. Dresses, blouses, trousers, have to be cut from fabric in the most economical way possible. This precludes the use of bold patterns with a spacious pattern repeat (which would involve wasting a part of the fabric in order to set the various pattern pieces so that they matched up attractively when stitched together). Even expensive ready-to-wear clothes are seldom made so that a stripe or a floral with a pronounced 'wave effect' is matched across the side seams, or across the bodice and sleeve seams. In extremely poor samples, the pattern is often not centred down the front of the garment.

The plaid dress, shown here, made by Poiret in 1925, is a stunning example of a patterned fabric used for the height of effect. The bodice section of the dress actually had a piece of the plaid pattern removed, so that the top half of the dress is in a smaller sequence of horizontal stripes, in comparison with the aproned skirt section. For added interest, the skirt aprons are ruched to add more life to a pattern that could be overwhelming if used completely flat (FIG 1).

ANALYSING A PATTERNED FABRIC

Using a bold pattern is an immediate way of adding distinction to your chosen style, and well worth the extra metrage or yardage that is sometimes required for pattern matching across the seams.

It is a way of creating a stunning affect simply: choose an easy pattern shape, but match bold motifs exactly and you have an instant impact.

First you must be able to see where the balance is placed in a design. Also take note if a fabric has a pronounced right and wrong side (which will affect your cutting out options), or whether it has a definite up and down imbalance or side-to-side imbalance. These last two points will help you to decide where the centre point of the pattern should fall on your dress or blouse, for example (**FIG 2A, 2B, 2C**).

FIG 1

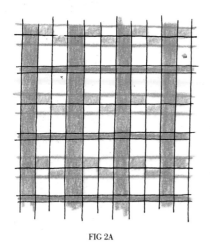

FIG 2A

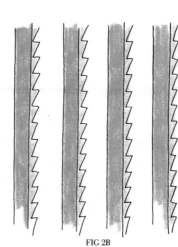

FIG 2B

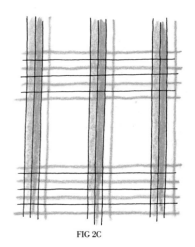

FIG 2C

TECHNIQUES FOR USING PATTERNED FABRICS

If a pattern is unbalanced vertically, then you must decide where the centre point of the pattern repeat falls, and use this for the centre point of the horizontal emphasis in your design. In a classic dress shape, this would fall across the hipline of the skirt, and across the bustline of the bodice. You should find a similar centre point to a pattern that is unbalanced side-to-side, and make this fall down the centre front of a blouse or dress. (Of course, there might be cases where the side-to-side pattern repeat is so wide, that a positive feature can be made of the fact by placing the pattern down one side of the garment. You could experiment with border-printed fabrics in this way.) (FIG 3A, 3B, 3C)

If the fabric has no right and wrong side, then matching the two halves of a bodice is easy to manage, simply by placing the pattern pieces side by side on exactly the same line of the fabric, and then reversing one piece. This method would work for a style that has a centre-front or back seam (centre-back being more common) (FIG 4A, 4B).

If you have to fold the fabric because there is a definite right and wrong side, then check that the fabric pieces are pinned very exactly together so that both halves of the fabric will be cut out along the same lines. The best method is to pin all over the fabric area to be cut out, keeping the top half of the fabric flapped back, matching the pattern sections bit by bit, and pinning through the two layers as you smooth the layers down flat together. Tack the fabric before cutting out (FIG 5).

FIG 3A

FIG 3B

FIG 3C

FIG 4A

FIG 4B

FIG 5

When you match a bodice or skirt section with a sleeve, you have the advantage, with commercial patterns, of little notches or numbered markings, on each pattern piece, which you can ensure fall on exactly the same point of the patterned fabric. The most important match is across the bodice front and the top half of the arm. Nothing is more unsightly than a badly matched sleeve seam – unless it is a badly matched skirt side seam, which 'screams' as it moves (FIG 6).

An alternative method to following the notch marks is to decide where the area of the pattern should fall on one section of the pattern piece, and trace over the design on to the paper pattern. (Make the trace *inside* the seam allowance.)

FIG 6

When this paper piece is moved in order to cut a second section, you will have the traced design permanently marked in order to place the pattern piece in exactly the same position on the fabric again. Be sure to match the patterns on the stitching line, not the edge of the seam allowance. This method is particularly useful if you are making a many-gored skirt, and have to juggle the position of the tissue pattern to make the most economical use of the fabric, while at the same time trying to maintain uniformity in the pattern position (FIG 7).

In the example illustrated, and in any other area where the joining seam is curved, or on a slant, it is impossible to keep the pattern matched up for the length of the seam. This is, of course, especially true of armholes, which have to be curved (though the eye is satisfied by a match where it counts the most – across the centre part of the armhole, as shown). Both sleeves have to be

FIG 7

FIG 9

FIG 10

FIG 8

matched very exactly on both sides, for a perfect finish. A flared skirt is difficult to match down the length of the seam, but a few key measurements across the hip area make all the difference to the overall finished effect (FIG 8).

COUTURIER DETAIL

As will be seen in the sketches showing examples of Poiret's work, he would often find ways to reduce the difficulties inherent in working with bold brightly patterned fabrics. Apart from his skill in matching or altering the dimensions of patterns, like the plaid dress, he would distract the eye from the difficulty of a join by inserting a piping cord into the seam, say at hip level. Alternatively, he might break areas of patterned fabric by using borders of another plainer material, often in a surprising colour, which had the effect of subduing and enriching a bold fabric – like the kimono design illustrated. Many of his designs with patterns would confront the problem by turning the fabric round – the sleeves might be cut on the bias rather than the up-and-down of a fabric (see page 40) (FIG 9).

If you decide to alter the direction of a fabric, say to cut a bodice section on the cross instead of the straight grain of the fabric, then the same rules about pattern matching on the seams can be made to apply – either using notched markings, or traced areas, as already described. Remember also to check that the central balancing line in the design does not appear drastically different when the fabric is laid on the cross, rather than the straight grain, and adjust the pattern pieces in position accordingly (FIG 10).

A statuesque Vionnet design, draped and sculpted, 1938.

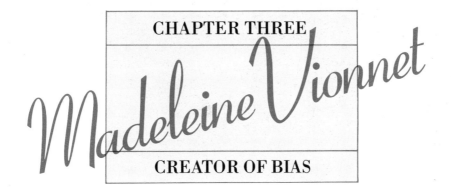

CHAPTER THREE

Madeleine Vionnet

CREATOR OF BIAS

Madeleine Vionnet was considered the doyenne of French dressmaking, not only because of her work, which was on a level of refinement hardly achieved by any other couturier, but also through her offices on behalf of the French fashion industry, and most particularly through her support of the Chambre Syndicale de la Couture Parisienne. Long after her retirement in 1939, she continued to be an active influence and force in Paris, advising colleges, inspiring students, and taking constant interest in the world over which she had reigned supreme for so long.

Her life began in 1877 in the village of Aubervilliers in the Jura, and as a child she showed a remarkable aptitude for study. Her favourite subject was mathematics, but as her father, a tax-collector himself, considered this an unsuitable pursuit for a girl, she reluctantly turned her interest to sewing. By some strange chemistry, she became obsessed with dressmaking and designing, so much so that at the tender age of 13 she left her village to become an apprentice dressmaker in the suburbs of Paris. An early and unsuccessful marriage in 1895 left her with a small baby, who died at six months. Perhaps because of these painful associations, she found the initiative to leave Paris for London, aged 18. Compared to many, she had already lived out a lifetime, but more was in store. The house she found to lodge in in London was run by a doctor who specialized in treating mentally disturbed patients – just at the time when psychiatry was in its infancy; this must have seemed strange indeed to Mlle Vionnet. But she was happy enough, and managed to secure work at the house of Kate Reilly, a well-known London dressmaker to Edwardian society. She stayed there for five years, becoming head of the workrooms, or *première* as it is termed in France.

Separation from her family (including a mother whom she barely knew) and no doubt the thought that she now had a training that would enable her to find better work, prompted her return to Paris. Vionnet's learning process continued, first at the house of Callot Soeurs, then enjoying

an enormous vogue, particularly with their elaborately shimmering, beaded evening dresses. She stayed here for five years. Vionnet then moved to the house of Doucet, who had been a leading couturier in his day, but who was now slightly out of keeping with the new era. He hoped that she would inject new life into his house, but the clientèle were somewhat set in their ways – used to whaleboned models, and formal outfits. By the middle of the first decade, Vionnet was aware that a new freedom was necessary, if not long overdue, and she found some outlet for her ideas in some exquisite lingerie work. Vionnet herself claimed, years later, that it was she, not Poiret, who threw off the rule of the corset during her years with Doucet, in 1907 to be precise. She also persuaded mannequins to show the dresses over their own skin, in bare feet, with sandals (as opposed to wearing the models over limb-encasing black crêpe foundations).

Whatever the truth of this claim (hotly contested like so many 'firsts' in couture history) and although most of Doucet's clients rejected her, Vionnet certainly managed to draw round herself an admiring group of some of the loveliest women in Paris, mostly from the demi-monde. These included notable actresses such as Marie Lecomte, Réjane and Eve Lavalière. One of the group, the actress Lanthelme, had such admiration for Vionnet's skill that she offered to set her up in a house of her own, but the plan was never realized. Lanthelme died in a drowning 'accident' thought by some to be suicide. By 1912, however, Vionnet had mustered a tiny sum, sufficient to enable her to leave Doucet and set up independently as a couturière in the rue Rivoli. It was an inauspicious opening, on the eve of war. Although she had talented help (notably Marcelle Chaumont who went on to open a house of her own), the venture floundered in a mass of unpaid bills and the House of Vionnet closed down. Despite the disappointment Vionnet secured jobs for all her staff – a gesture of loyalty well repaid, for in 1918 when she re-opened, (the husband of a leading beauty and socialite, Mme Martinez de Hoz, provided her

above _Madeleine Vionnet,
unbelievable as it now
seems, the first couturier to
design a dress that pulled on
over the head and the first to
use crêpe de chine for a dress
rather than only for a coat
lining. She brought a new
soft, draped look to clothes._

left _Two designs that show
Vionnet's radical departure
from previous rules of
dressmaking. Simple, easy-
to-wear but still very
glamorous. Women were
beginning to have their
practical requirements met
but still had to look
decorative, and overtly
feminine. (c. 1929.)_

above _An ensemble that
reveals the easy grace of
Vionnet's designs. The large
collar adds definition to a
very fluid, simple shape.
Vionnet's clothes could be
worn by real women, not
just by the ideally-
proportioned figure. Her
bias cut was essential for
that. July 1937._

with more substantial finance), they all returned to her.

Vionnet's contribution to couture came from her firm belief that 'fashion' as such was the pursuit of very few women. New styles suited only a handful of ladies – those with the right frame and looks to epitomize the style of the moment. For the majority, subtle variations of the vogue had to be found, that would enable them to be beautiful in an individual way. To achieve the new freedom, Vionnet made a simple innovation: she commissioned fabric two yards wider than the norm, so that she could drape the material round the body, to its fullest extent, and make a new, dramatic use of the bias cut. In so doing, she created a modern version of a Grecian silhouette. If her intention was to create clothes that were thoroughly individualized, in one sense she failed. The beauty of her dresses was that almost any figure could be made stunning wearing them. In her own words:

> One must examine the anatomy of every customer. The dress must not hang on the body but follow its lines. It must accompany its wearer and when a woman smiles the dress must smile with her. The direction of the material, the weave and the cross lines on the one hand; precision, cut, proportion and balance on the other – that is what I oppose to the term fashion, which is an empty word and completely meaningless to a real dressmaker.

By 1923 Vionnet was able to move to bigger quarters in the Avenue Montaigne and her staff increased to over 1000. The richest women in the world, the Queen of Spain, Queen Elizabeth of Belgium, the Rothschilds, Mme Clemenceau, Mme Citroen and Mrs Harrison Williams were all constant patrons. Throughout the period up to the outbreak of the Second World War, she worked diligently, relentlessly even, in a stream of creativity unrivalled by her colleagues in the field. She designed her dresses by working with small dolls or mannequins, cutting out slips of fabric in the round, as it is termed, and working strictly with the feel and fall of the cloth. People who watched spoke enthusiastically of the exciting scene, when, like a sculptor, she modelled and draped in search of new harmonies. She said herself, 'I have discovered a system of cutting, and have ended up by becoming a slave to my own system'.

Observing her dresses today in detail, it is easy to see why Jacques Worth thought her the greatest technician of modern Haute Couture. The seams are so finely balanced, so perfectly and minutely stitched that they barely interfere with the rippling soft movement of the cloth. They were uncopiable: dresses had to be unpicked and laid flat to be understood. Not all her designs were satin, or crêpe de chine robes: she could work equal magic with wools and gaberdines. When built-up shoulders made their appearance in day wear in 1933, she produced versions of the look which had no pads, but merely a draped shoulder line. According to Madeleine Ginsburg, head of the Victoria and Albert Museum's costume department, none of these drape dresses have survived for further study, but from photographs they appear both graceful and effective. Vionnet also made particularly dramatic use of stripes and plaids, again using her eye for diagonals and bias lines, to decorate collars, gilets, and provide unusual variations of the new suit, much favoured in the early thirties, with skirts in darker, differing colours from the jackets. When stiffer, wider-skirted styles seemed to be returning in the autumn of 1934, she had the courage to scrap an entire collection in time to start again, producing clothes that captured the mood of the moment to perfection, including not soft-draped satins but wide-skirted taffetas.

In spite of such reversals, Vionnet learned to be a good businesswoman as well as a supreme artist, often in combination. Once (according to Caroline Seebohm, Condé Nast's biographer), one of her favourite customers, Leone Blakemore Moats, a well-known American hostess, asked the couturière why she charged her so little for her clothes, 90 to 110 dollars for a day dress, 110 to 150 dollars for an evening gown, roughly half the price for the times. Vionnet's answer seems to sum up her aims: to dress women whose personal style she enjoyed, in a manner becoming to them, and at the same time, to survive:

> First, I am an artist and it is a joy to have my work understood and set off to its best advantage. The second is because I am a businesswoman, and you are a good advertizement. I know that when you go to a Sunday dinner dance at the Ritz at least three women who see you there will be at my door on Monday morning asking for the model you wore.

In 1939 the expiration of her lease and increasing years decided her to retire, although her influence continued through the work of her protégés, Marcelle Chaumont, Mad Carpentier and Jacques Griffe.

Madeleine Vionnet's method of working was radical and changed the look of women's dresses completely. It is interesting to note that the women designers of Paris were often the ones who created an ease and wearability in clothes, whereas the male couturiers were more interested in a 'look', sometimes immobilizing women in the process!

Modelling in the round, as Vionnet did, is a matter of working out the design for a dress from a clear idea in the head, or in a sketch, and translating that into reality by forming a muslin toile or first version of the design, by pulling, folding, and draping the fabric, on a three-dimensional figure. Vionnet worked with small mannequin-like dolls. Other designers or tailoring students work with a life-like dummy. Fabric is flat – bodies are rounded and curved. To obtain a shape that fits a body and looks natural, the fabric must be curved, by various means, to take a volume in form. When a designer works from a sketch or an idea, certain essentials must emerge quickly: where the main

seams will be, where the main emphasis of the draping line will fall. Having decided on this, the muslin fabric will be pinned up against the dummy, and the fullness of the fabric 'suppressed', that is pinned, darted and cut away, so that the cloth begins to take on the body form, while the position of the seam lines emphasize the idea of the garment desired by the designer. A feature of couture design is, obviously, an elaborate construction, for this is the one luxury that ready-to-wear clothes cannot supply. A successful combination of unusual cut and seaming with totally individualized fit gives custom-made clothes their personality.

Modelling a toile is a very complicated business. It takes many years of practice (besides a great measure of natural aptitude) to perfect, and is not something that can be learnt from a book, but only through experience. However, the principles of transforming something flat into a shape with volume and form are not so difficult to grasp and will help you to adapt your own patterns.

CREATING 'SHAPE'

There are obvious places, in the design of a classic shape for the female form, where the fullness of the material is 'suppressed' or taken out of the fabric, so that a rounded shape is achieved.

Most dress designs hang from the shoulder seam: sometimes darting (taking out fullness) is needed at the neck and on the shoulder seam itself, depending on the shape of the bodice or sleeve. The fabric is moulded over the bust, involving more darting (taking out of fullness again) under the arm, under the bust, or in the side bodice seam. The basic seamlines are important to understand, even if only in theory, because when you decide to adapt a pattern or make it fit better, you should work always on the main seam lines, known as the 'fitting seams', rather than take away or let out the dimensions in a seam, which is merely a decorative elaboration.

It is also essential to remember that when you take the fullness out of one area of a pattern – say if you happen to be small-busted, or small-hipped, then a certain distortion

in the pattern piece may result, and you may need to let out fabric in another direction, so that the piece lies true.

The same principle applies to altering patterns, as the examples given here illustrate. In order to create the fullness required in the front section of a bodice for gathers over the chest bone, for example, the fullness is taken from the shoulder, by removing the dart line from the basic blouse shape. This is why the term 'suppression' is used: the shaping required in translating a piece of flat, flexible cloth into a three-dimensional form, means that fullness must appear *somewhere*, and must be brought into use in exactly the right spot.

An alternative way of dealing with the creation of three-dimensionality in a form, is to use less structure, and rely on the moulding qualities of the bias in certain fabrics such as jerseys, satins, silks, certain cotton lawns, etc. This is essentially what Vionnet chose to do. These fabrics have greater elasticity, greater moulding powers when strained across the grain, than when

under tension along the grain. A bias-cut fabric moulds to the body in a completely different manner to a straight-grain fabric such as firm-woven wool. Bias-cut dresses have a soft suppleness that is unmistakable. Fullness emerges from a soft sleekness. The best example of this is a flared skirt, which sits loosely but close over the hips, and descends into full flares over the thighs, while retaining a plastic, moulding quality that fabrics cut on the straight grain do not reveal.

The following are samples of ways of dealing with 'fullness' to create designs that are very 1930s in feel, and re-create the look which Vionnet perfected.

BODICE WITH GATHERS AT THE FRONT

A very simple demonstration of the principle of fullness, and the need to 'suppress' it while forming a three-dimensional shape comes from this easy adaptation of a blouse pattern to give gathers at the neck of a dress, a very 'thirties' conception.

Choose a basic blouse pattern with a long centre-front dart, as illustrated. Close the dart in the paper pattern itself. This will automatically cause a buckling of the paper – a form in volume. Cut across the centre-front line, as shown, to the end point of the darts. The paper now lies flat. This is the area that will create gathers, i.e. take up the fullness of the bodice front. The centre-front seam, from the waist up to the cutting line on the paper pattern, can be laid against the fold of the bodice-front fabric, but the gathered area will require a centre-front seam. Allow an extra 1.5cm (⅝in) to the pattern edge, at the neck, for the seaming (FIG 1).

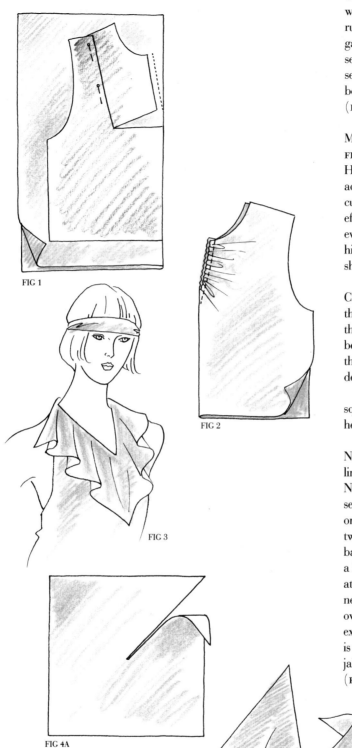

FIG 1

FIG 2

FIG 3

FIG 4A

FIG 4B

Gather up the centre edges first, with double rows of very fine running stitches. Arrange the gathers either side of the centre seam line and then stitch this seam in place. Make up the bodice front in the usual way (FIG 2).

MAKING A JABOT FOR A BLOUSE FRONT OR DRESS

Here is a very simple adaptation of the use of bias cutting, which could make an effective addition to day or evening wear. It could fit over a high square or round-necked shape.

Cut a square of soft fabric, with the diagonal measuring double the length of the measurement between the centre-front, at the throat, to the base of the length desired for the jabot (FIG 3).

Neaten the four edges of the square (see page 122 for hemming fine fabrics).

Now cut through the diagonal line to the centre of the square. Neaten the two edges of this seam, either with bias binding or very fine hand-rolling. The two points that form the centre-back can be finished either with a button and loop, or can be attached to the back centre neckline of the dress or blouse – overlapping the zip placket, for example. Light hand-stitching is used to apply the front of the jabot to the front of the bodice (FIG 4A, 4B).

OTHER CASCADES, DRAPES AND FRILLS

Falling drapes were great features of Vionnet's thirties dresses. The simplest are easy to achieve: cut an oblong of fabric to the width required for the fall, plus seam allowances. (This cascade would look best mounted into a centre-front seam, or an off-centre seam.) When attached, the cascade falls attractively into fluted shapes (FIG 5A, 5B, 5C).

A more dramatic frill can be made by cutting a curved strip of fabric, as illustrated, and marking the front section of a skirt pattern piece with the positioning, as shown. In this case, the frill must be neatened with machine zigzag or hand stitching and mounted on to the right side of the skirt front, as shown (FIG 6A, 6B, 6C).

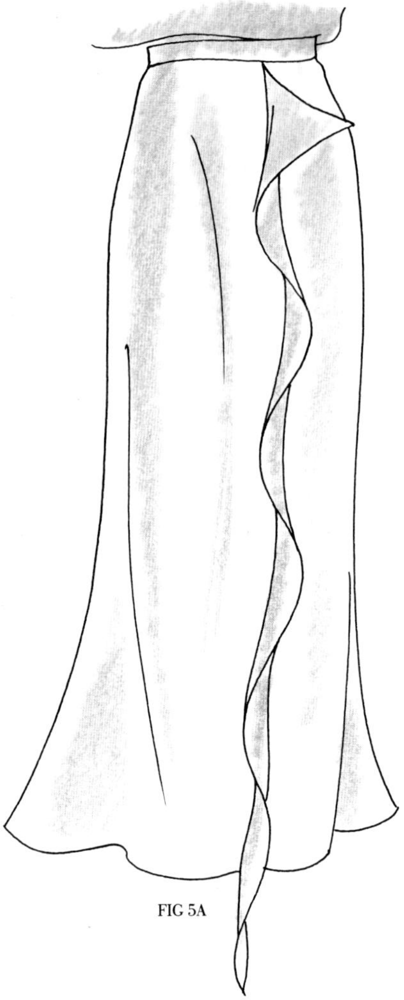

FIG 5A

FIG 5B

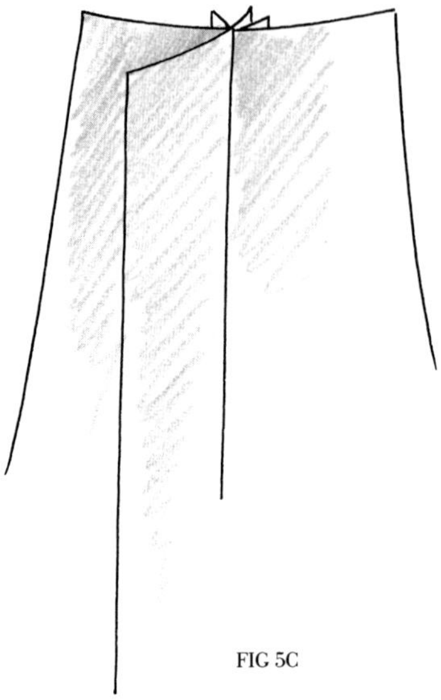

FIG 5C

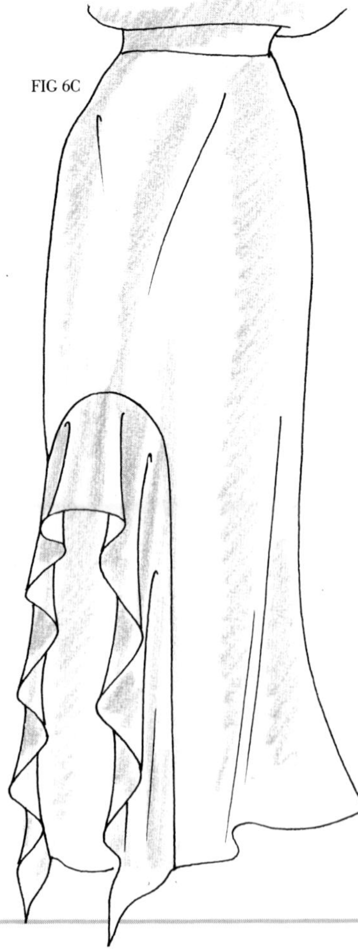

FIG 6C

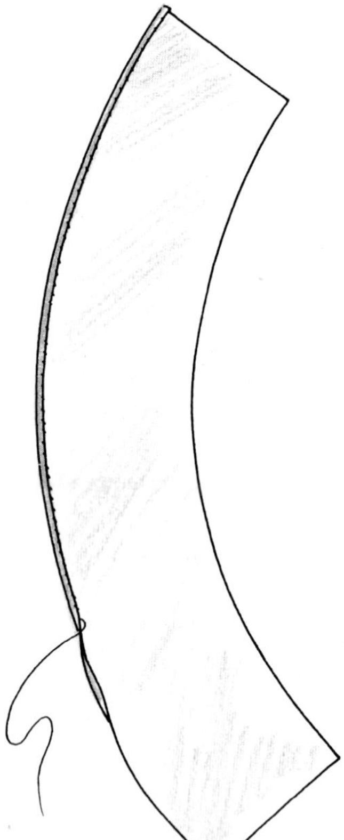

FIG 6A

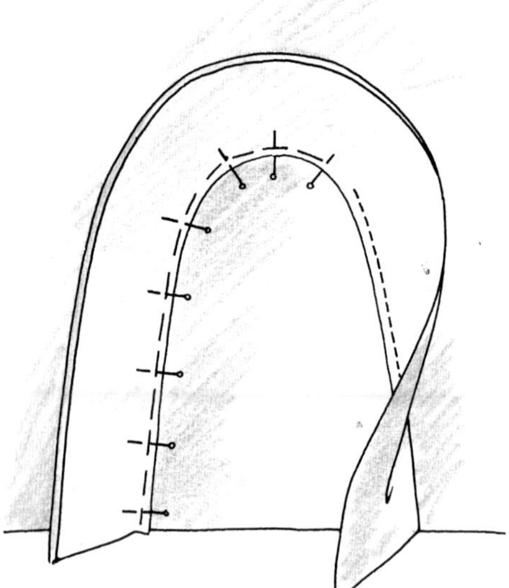

FIG 6B

A variation on the cascade is a shaped frill, the fullness coming from the 'opening out' of the basic shape in order to get the fluted draping. This design is actually much easier to achieve than it at first appears, and once the concept is clear, any number of variations could be achieved. For a curved skirt frill, mark the line on a basic skirt shape actually on the paper pattern, where the frill will be positioned (FIG 7).

Now place a piece of tissue paper over the skirt paper pattern, on the diagonal as shown, and mark the lines where the extra fullness for the cascades will be required. Make sure that you draw the parallel lines for the fullness exactly as indicated, following the shaping lines of the skirt flare and not along the dotted lines (FIG 8).

Once the curving pattern piece has been drawn and covered with the parallel lines, remove it, cut it out, and then slit the flare lines, opening them out to the fullness required for the cascades. Follow the simple instructions for mounting the cascades as shown in the previous example (FIG 9).

FIG 7

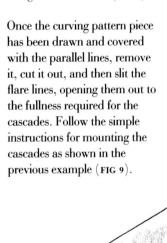

FIG 9

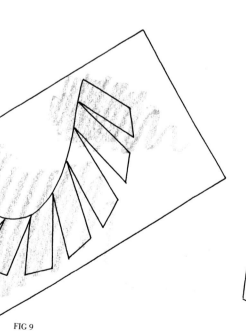

FIG 8

The Schiaparelli look: mannish shapes, witty detail. The 'Shoe' hat, Autumn 1938.

CHAPTER FOUR

Elsa Schiaparelli

SURREALIST IN FASHION

Elsa Schiaparelli called her autobiography *Shocking Life* and it was published with a bright pink cover – the 'hot' pink with which she is always associated. The words and the colour sum up her impact on Paris couture in the thirties: she was an endless innovator, and a brilliant colourist. Chanel described her as: 'The Italian artist who makes dresses'. Although this was said in a derogatory tone, the phrase can be seen as a compliment, a valid assessment of Schiaparelli's work. She did not excel in the superb drapery, the originality of cut and concept found in other couturiers such as Vionnet or later, Balenciaga, and it is not at all clear from her memoirs whether she knew much about cutting and sewing herself. But it is evident that she had a demanding eye for detail, adored decoration of all kinds (but particularly buttons) and often invented new fashions by simply taking a radical approach to the garment and the situation for which it was required.

Schiaparelli was born in Rome to a very distinguished aristocratic, academic family. She grew up in exquisitely beautiful surroundings, the Palazzo Corsini in the Trastevere, next to the Biblioteca dell'Academia dei Lincei, a specialist private library of which her father was curator. Schiaparelli had a difficult childhood, for she was plain, rebellious, and very intelligent – not at all suitable attributes in those days for a marriageable girl of her class. In her late teens she shocked her family by producing a slim volume of verse, *Arethusa*, which was very well reviewed and received a great deal of publicity both within and outside Italy. Elsa's family was scandalized, and she was sent to a convent in Germany as punishment.

As often happens to girls of her temperament, Elsa made an unsuitable marriage as an escape from her family. On a trip to England she met and married a part-Breton, part-Polish, minor aristocrat, Count William de Kerlor. The marriage barely lasted for the duration of the war: by the year of the 1918 Armistice, Elsa Schiaparelli was living alone, in New York, with a small sickly child to support,

deserted by her husband. To return to Italy was unthinkable: the loss of freedom and the inevitable recriminations were not to her liking. Fortunately, her stay in New York enabled her to make some very useful friends, who helped her to find lodgings and eke out a living. One, Blanche Hays, financed her return to Europe, to Paris, and Elsa set about the business of making a living for herself and her daughter, Gogo.

By chance, through rich American friends, Schiaparelli met the great Paul Poiret, who was so taken by her unusual somewhat pre-Raphaelite looks that he gave her a magnificent coat (made, typically for him, of upholstery velvet) and in the course of the next months showered her with other gifts of gorgeous clothes, out of keeping with her life style but all the same adored. Through Poiret, Schiaparelli met the artistic world of Paris, and this no doubt led to her growing confidence in herself. As she described in her own book:

> Once or twice I had thought that instead of painting or sculpture, both of which I did fairly well, I could invent dresses or costumes. Dress designing, incidentally, is to me not a profession but an art. I found that it was a most difficult and unsatisfying art, because as soon as a dress is born it has already become a thing of the past . . .

Schiaparelli's first sortie into the world of fashion has become a legend. She met another rich American, a woman friend who happened to be wearing an unusually knitted sweater – jerseys at the time had become high fashion pieces. The sweater had been hand-made by an Armenian peasant woman living in Paris. Schiaparelli went to see her, and quickly drew a design to be commissioned:

> I drew a large butterfly bow in front, like a scarf around the neck – the primitive drawing of a child in prehistoric times. I said: "The bow must be white against a black ground, and there will be white underneath." On the third attempt, the Armenian lady got it right.

above *Schiaparelli in typical extrovert mood at a Carnival party, 1952.*

right *Harper's Bazaar, 1900, showing the freshness of Schiaparelli's designs, 1948.*

Schiaparelli wore the knitted jumper to a smart lunch and caused a furore. Her very first order was for 40 sweaters and 40 skirts for the New York store, Strauss.

Typically, the fairy-tale numbering appealed to Schiaparelli's sense of daring and she at once said yes, having no idea how to knit up a skirt or even order one. Soon, Schiaparelli's work load increased so that she could open a small workroom-cum-apartment at 4 rue de la Paix. In 1935 she was able to move to more generous quarters in the Place Vendôme – in fact she bought a house there, number 21, from the now elderly couturier, Mme Chéruit.

Schiaparelli knew little about sewing but she did know about line and proportion, mainly from her studies in Rome, and more instinctively from her background in fine palaces and beautiful squares. She decided:

Clothes have to be architectural: the body must never be forgotten and it must be used as a frame is used in a building. The vagaries of lines and details or any asymmetric effect must always have a close connection with this frame. The more the body is respected, the better the dress acquires vitality.

Schiaparelli's designs for dresses were always witty, unusual, even crazy, but they were always smart and sophisticated. She attracted a very expensive clientèle –

socialites, bankers' wives, personalities like Amy Johnson, actresses like Arletty. Ina Claire, the American film star bought a strange knitted tube of a cap, popularized it, so that it was copied by an American manufacturer, nicknamed the Mad Cap, and made a fortune. Such incidents were to happen time and time again to Schiaparelli, who (unlike Chanel) hardly cared about the copying, in spite of the great revenue she lost by the pirating of her ideas.

Apart from her inventiveness, Schiaparelli had an artist's love of colour and texture in materials. She collaborated in inventing new substances. An American contract that resulted from her first couture collection was with the firm of Westcott Hosiery Mills, using 'Fabrimode' – stockings and garment fabric made to give the same effect, whether silk, crêpe chiffon, shantung, tweed. She confused the traditional uses of fabrics: wool in place of silk, mattress ticking in place of linen, and often mixed different textures in a way not seen previously: velvet with satin, fabric and fur such as tweed and leopard skin. She was always alive to new possibilities: rayon, for example, invented in 1920 by the French fabric manufacturers, Colcombet, appealed to her enormously and she used it in many forms to imitate silks, wools, crêpes and cottons. Another extraordinary substance she liked was cellophane, because of its soft shine. The Colcombet firm created a cellophane and synthetic silk mixture called 'Balboa' in 1932 which she used for her designs. In 1934 this was followed by her famous glass tunics – clothes made of glass fibre fabric, known as Rhodophane.

Two other aspects of her work are unmistakable signatures of her talent. One was her adoption of the new zipper in 1935. Typically, instead of concealing it, she had plastic zippers dyed to match the colouring of her fabrics, and set the zippers in exposed positions, for all to see. Her collection in the autumn of that year was quite esoteric – 'tweeds for the evening, padlocks for suits, evening raincoats, glass dresses, and buttons of golden sovereigns and French Louis to mock the next French devaluation'.

When several of her new zipper dresses were sent to America, they were at first refused entry, due to some protectionist agreement between the two countries to prevent zippers from being imported. But Schiaparelli protested with her customary vigour to the authorities, and at last gained entry. Ever after, like Columbus, they were certain of their arrival.

Buttons, however, never lost their appeal to her. In her famous circus collection in 1938, buttons were made in the shape of acrobats, diving down the front of a silk brocade jacket, decorated with roundabout horses. Another set were made to look like fairy-tale handmirrors, each one at least six or seven inches in length. She used wood, plexiglass, feathers, chains – any substance whatsoever to give life and amusement to her clothes. Schiaparelli collaborated with the best artistic talent of her day – Jean Schlumberger for her buttons, Jean Clément for her costume jewellery, Salvador Dali, Christian Bérard and Jean Cocteau for fabric prints and embroideries.

BRUYÈRE

CHRISTIAN DIOR

ROBERT PIGUET

HENRY A LA PENSÉE

MARCEL ROCHAS

SCHIAPARELLI

left *Schiaparelli's decorative details often had a surreal element, echoed by the clever arrangement of this picture by Cecil Beaton. The workmanship in her embroidered and beaded clothing was extraordinary for a couturier who liked to be irreverent and witty.*

right *Unusual, popular prints were a feature of Schiaparelli's designs. She managed to make even beach and sunwear highly fashion-conscious. Her taste for casual clothes shows a move towards more egalitarian styles.*

Every trip that Schiaparelli undertook during the thirties provided her with inspiration. Skiing in Switzerland caused her to design thick jumpers with padded square shoulders; a trip to the Tyrol inspired peasant fashion; similarly, she plundered the folk designs and colourways of North Africa, Peru, Mexico, and Russia. This internationalism was an unusual aspect of her work as a couturier.

Not for a moment should it be thought that Schiaparelli's clothes achieved their effect through dashing design alone. She was thorough and demanding about her work, and had the shrewdness to surround herself with excellent professionals. She hired only the best people to work with her. When she opened her rue de la Paix showroom, two vendeuses from Patou were soon followed by one of his best tailors.

One well-preserved model, in the collection at the Museum of Costume in Bath, an evening dress made in mauve-blue charmeuse in 1936, evidences her care for detail. The body of the fabric of a full-length princess line dress, heavily encrusted with a necklet of fine pearlwork at the neck, was hand-stitched with pearl and silver embroideries, in the shape of crossed keys. Six of the motifs are identical, running down the front of the dress, but the two off-centre designs, falling at knee level, are slightly smaller, altered versions of the motif, in order to create a perfect balance in the overall design. The dress has a machine-stitched plastic zip at the back of the neck, set wide so that the big teeth are all displayed, but the zip is dyed blue to match the fabric, and a tiny bar of fabric is hand-stitched across the inside of the head of the zipper, to prevent the plastic from sitting uncomfortably on the back neckbone of the wearer.

Another example of her work, an evening jacket (now in a private collection in New York) covered in green and pink flowers and leaves in fine organza, each one separately stitched to the fabric, was so exquisitely executed that the flowerets were continued up under the collar of the jacket, where normally they would hardly be exposed to view – presumably so that the wearer could lift the collar slightly and still present a perfectly finished decoration. Stringent care for detail is a hallmark of her work – however throwaway and witty the concept may superficially appear to be, it is always painstakingly executed.

During the war years, Schiaparelli felt unable to continue to work in Paris, occupied as it was by the Germans. She decided to do what she could to promote the idea of Paris as an everlasting citadel of the couture industry, and did much to keep the flag flying by lecturing, touring various cities of America, and publicizing the work of the French fashion world, at the same time raising money for refugee children in the Free Zone area of southern France. She took with her a collection of clothes, which unfortunately was lost when the ship transporting them was sunk in the Atlantic in 1940. Schiaparelli had to re-make her collection in the workrooms of Bonwit Teller, and had an interesting comment to make on the differences she discovered between French and American work.

It is much more difficult to produce an original collection in America than in our country because here we have unlimited materials on approval, whilst in America these materials have to be bought, and if on second thoughts they are not suitable, or if one changes one's mind, one is confronted with a flat loss. Moreover, a detail like a button, unless made in vast quantities, takes on the importance and the price of a jewel.

Something came out of this work in the end, but the collection proved frightfully expensive and in spite of the genuine goodwill and ability of the workers, not quite what I wanted.

In spite of these difficulties, Schiaparelli's tour was a great success (she ended by addressing no fewer than 26,000 people in St Paul Minnesota) and Schiaparelli herself was always an adored favourite with wealthy American patrons. She understood how to design new ideas in clothes to suit an untraditional clientele: cocktail aprons to match dinner dresses, trouser outfits for women who had to drive themselves rather than be chauffeured and take care of their own homes and gardens, simplified underwear, blouses and skirts, without the need for complicated lace and silk underpinnings and linings – all these ideas were liberating and forward-looking.

Schiaparelli went back to continue her work in Paris at the end of the war, but never regained the assurance that distinguished her designing during the thirties. It is no accident that the designer who caught the mood of women at the end of the war was Dior – a man who had a completely different vision of womanhood from Elsa, who dressed, basically, women with an atmosphere like herself: sophisticated, independent, given to making an effect rather than interested in presenting a quiet femininity. By the middle fifties, her couture business was deeply in debt, and she was forced to show for the last time in 1954. True to her fierce independence, she succeeded in paying off all her creditors with the profits of her perfumery business. She continued to be an immensely popular personality frequently appearing in fashion magazines, making personal appearances to promote her perfumes, and leading an active social life until her death in 1973.

Anny Latour, in her book on the French couturiers, *Kings of Fashion*, passes a rather harsh judgement on Schiaparelli, suggesting that she reigned supreme in an era with a 'general loss of style', an age 'constantly in search of new sensations'. Others have derided Schiaparelli's claim to be fascinated by the body, and to desire to dress it architecturally, because she 'masculinized' the silhouette with high padded shoulders, narrow waists and elongated hiplines. But Schiaparelli brought great originality and invention into clothes and expanded the borders of the acceptable. She was an instinctive feminist – which can be interpreted as meaning that she explored the masculine side of women's image of themselves. She also had the strength of character to make fun of the overly serious aspects of couture work, with her gigantic buttons and surreal pockets.

One of the features of Schiaparelli's clothes that gives them wit and distinction is her use of all kinds of closures for buttons and zips, and her unorthodox positioning of pockets. Although the preparation of buttonholes and pockets can be time-consuming, the effort is repaid in the most characterful results. Here are four basic techniques of tailoring that repay every minute of effort. A word of warning though: a practice run, on a spare piece of the actual fabric that you intend to use is invaluable, so that you learn how to handle its bulk, its fraying rate, and perfect your stitching on the cloth. Schiaparelli's tailors would have so many years of experience (with probably one person specializing in buttonholing exclusively) that they would adjust their stitching to any fabric they encountered. Such sensitivity takes years to acquire: experimenting with each individual sample at least prevents you from ruining the garment currently in hand.

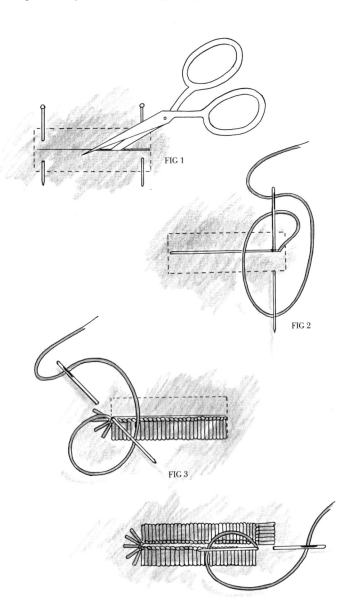

FIG 1

FIG 2

FIG 3

POSITIONING BUTTONHOLES

The position of buttonholes on a garment is largely a matter of taste but there are certain fundamentals that you can use to test your eye. The buttonhole itself should be marked to allow for the width of the button, plus 3mm (⅛in) towards the inner edge of the front opening. The top button of a classic round-necked top should be placed roughly half the width of the button _down_ from the top edge.

For blouses and tight fitting jackets, you may find it easier to work out the positioning from the mid-point of the bust line – nothing looks worse than a gap over the bust. Button size should be related to the cut of the jacket or blouse, and to the weight of the fabric.

While pretty large buttons may look attractive in abstract, they may pull too much in reality on a lightweight fabric, and ruin the design.

WORKED BUTTONHOLES

Old fashioned tailors would often run their threads through a block of beeswax to give it extra smoothness, when being pulled through fabric. Although modern threads are highly polished, and suggest that such a precaution is unnecessary, it may prove helpful to experiment with a block of beeswax, to see if this gives the thread the extra firmness required for you to work a buttonhole well.

Mark the lines for the positions of the buttonholes with tailor's chalk, pins or basting threads. Check several times, fitting the garment, so that no mistakes are made! Worked buttonholes call for cutting the fabric, an irreversible step. Once pinned, using extremely sharp small scissors, slit the fabric to the width of the button. Make a row of small running stitches round the area of the buttonhole, not only to hold any lining or interfacing exactly in place, but also to act as a guide for the depth of the buttonholing stitches (FIG 1).

Snip again using those exceedingly sharp scissors, through the middle area of the buttonhole, exactly on the required line for its position. A most important step: carefully oversew round the cut edge of the buttonhole, taking care not to pull on the fabric, or cause it to curl in any way. This is the most vital step towards the success of good buttonhole working. Start working in buttonhole stitch, on the wrong side of the cloth, at the top edge away from the opening (FIG 2).

Work round to the opposite end, making the buttonhole stitches fan out evenly and ensuring that they are the same length as the stitches already worked round the two sides of the buttonhole. Work the second side as the first. Complete the opposite end to the rounded end with long stitches, exactly double the length of the buttonhole stitches already worked. Make three or four of these, depending on the thickness of the fabric and the thread used (FIG 3).

Now work stitches horizontally around these vertical stitches, making sure to catch up the fabric underneath, to make a tight bar, protecting the edging of the buttonhole. Finish the thread off neatly on the wrong side of the buttonhole.

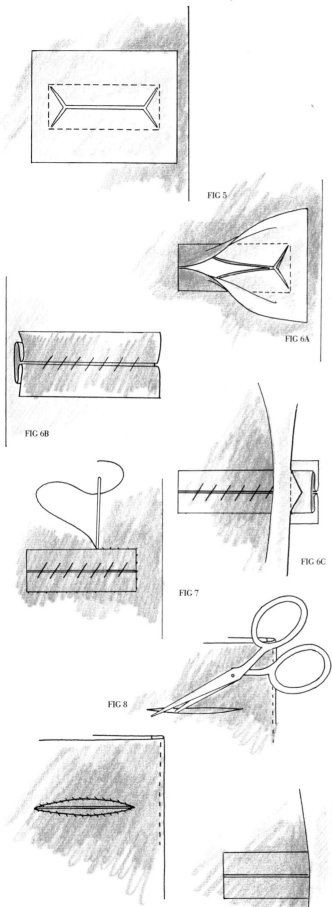

FIG 5

FIG 6A

FIG 6B

FIG 6C

FIG 7

FIG 8

COVERED BUTTONHOLES

Covered buttonholes are difficult to make, but once perfected transform the appearance of hand-made clothing, and are both attractive and durable. It is advisable to try them out first with tight-woven fabrics, which are not too thick. Pulling through the small scrap that creates the binding will otherwise present difficulties.

Mark the position of the buttonholes as previously explained. Cut a small patch of fabric, either the same as the garment cloth, or in a similar weight contrast colour, for an exotic detail to the finishing. The patch should be roughly 5cm (2in) longer than the area to be worked as the buttonhole, and it should also extend 1cm (½in) beyond the ends of it. Place it on the right side of the fabric, right sides together, baste and then work very small running stitches, 2mm (⅛in) long around the cutting line for the buttonhole.

Count the stitches so that you make exactly the same number, on both sides and at both ends of the buttonhole. Regularity is essential. (You can machine stitch, but handworking gives extra flexibility and accuracy.) Now cut down the centre line of the buttonhole, to within 0.5cm (¼in) of each end and make small v-shaped incisions into each corner of the stitched area, as shown in the diagram (FIG 5).

Gently push the patch of fabric through the slit, to the wrong side. Then, very carefully form a small inverted pleat on the back of the buttonhole. Hand-stitch a few times across each end of the buttonhole, through the pleat, to hold it in place, making sure these stitches catch into the v-shaped piece underneath. Using steam, press the folded back of the buttonhole in place (FIG 6A, 6B, 6C).

If desired, baste the pleated edge of the buttonhole opening closed, until the buttonhole is completed. Then turn the buttonhole to the right side, and fix the buttonhole edging firmly in place by stab stitching through the fold, exactly in the seamline, as shown (FIG 7).

These vertical stitches should disappear into the seamline and hardly remain visible. The edges of the pleated patch are concealed inside the facing. Once mounted, pinned and basted in position, merely slit the facing directly behind the buttonhole line, curve the edges of the fabric in with the fingernail, and then work very fine hemstitches round the edge of the turning, to finish (FIG 8).

CORDED BUTTONHOLES

A pronounced finish can be made by threading soft cotton cording through the pleats forming the buttonhole, to give a raised, chunky look. The ends of the cord are trimmed off and hand-stitched over, at each end of the pleat-folds, before the facing is applied and hand-stitched also (FIG 9).

FIG 9

MAKING A WELT POCKET

Working to the dimensions of your choice, cut out the welt piece and a matching piece of interfacing, which should be half the width of the welt, plus 1.5cm (⅝in) over the centre fold line. First baste the interfacing in place on the wrong side of the fabric: next trim away the three outer seam allowances, and then make a small fine line of running stitches just outside the centre fold line of the welt piece, as illustrated. (This extra piece of interfacing, when folded inside the welt, gives strength and fineness to the top edge of the finished pocket.) Now fold the welt piece in half, and baste down in place. Machine-stitch the two ends of the welt, and turn the piece through to the right side. (Push out the corner very squarely with the ends of a pair of closed scissors.) Steam press flat without stretching (**FIG 10A, 10B**).

Trim half the seam allowance away from the remaining unstitched long edge. Apply any decorative stitching to the folded edge and the two short ends (see page 94 for topstitching) (**FIG 11**).

Next check the placing of the welt on the garment. Mark the centre line, exactly where the pocket will be placed, with a line of small basting stitches, and mark two further lines, one above, one below, matching exactly the remaining seam allowance area of the folded welt. Pin the welt so that the raw edges correspond exactly to the slashing line, and the seamlines match up accordingly, then baste in place. Finally, stitch along the welt seamline. Finish off the thread ends by stitching them in by hand (**FIG 12**).

To add a pocket lining, cut out the shape of the pocket on a folded piece of cloth, pin and then baste in place, right sides together, as shown. Mark exactly the same three lines (slash line, and two seamlines, above and below). Stitch along the two outer lines, above and below the slash line, but not across the two ends. (All this can be done by hand, which produces a softer, stronger, more flexible form of stitching.) (**FIG 13**)

Now cut through the slash line with a very sharp pair of scissors, making v-shaped incisions into the four corners, as illustrated, and at the same time cutting into the actual fabric of the garment. Next, very carefully ease the two halves of the pocket lining through the slit, to the wrong side of the body fabric (**FIG 14**).

Fold the upper pocket down over the under-pocket lining, and neaten the slashed edges of the lining by hand, with close oversewing stitches. Machine or hand-stitch round the three sides of the pocket pieces, aligning them exactly. (Be sure to catch the little cut triangles into the side-seams, as these will hold the pocket turned inwards at right angles to the slash line, very accurately.) The seamed edges of the pocket can be oversewn to finish them, or bound with a very light bias binding, if the fabric itself is thick enough to allow for this extra treatment, without a ridge appearing in the surface of the finished garment. (This would work on heavy tweed coats or pinafore dresses, but not silks or lightweight wools). Some welt pockets are lined in self fabric, others in good quality, hardwearing material. (**FIG 15**).

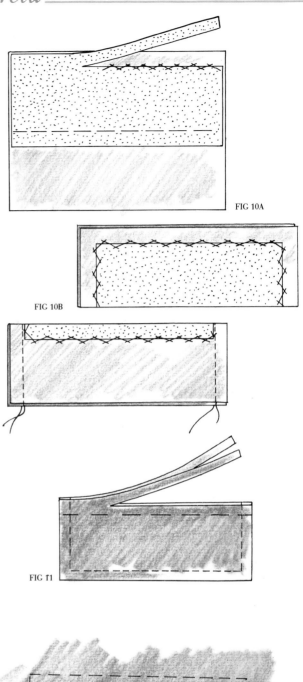

FIG 10A

FIG 10B

FIG 11

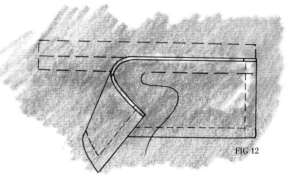

FIG 12

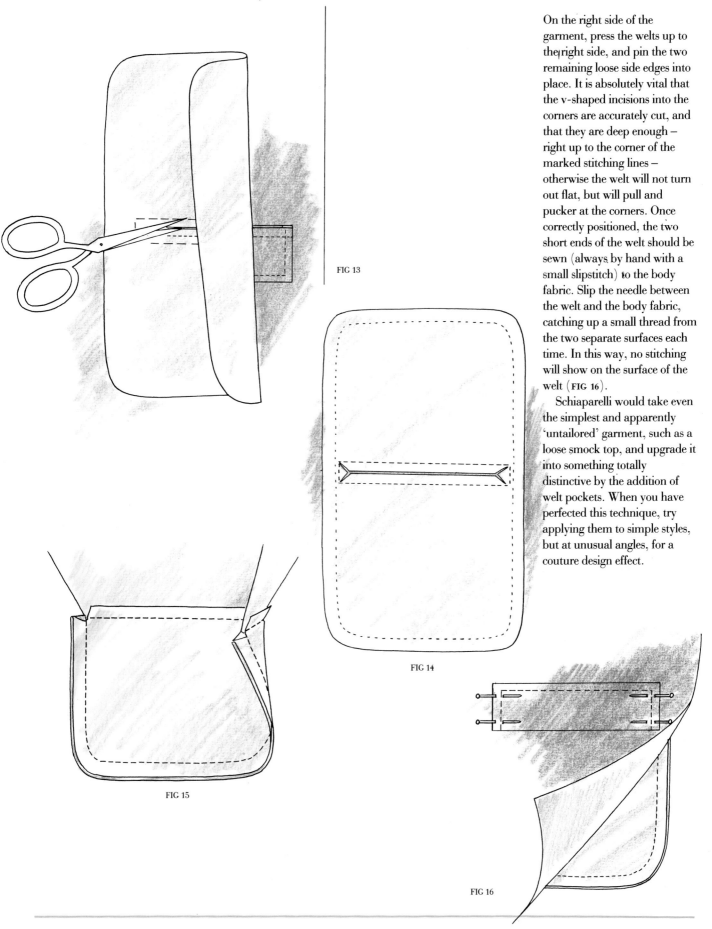

On the right side of the garment, press the welts up to the right side, and pin the two remaining loose side edges into place. It is absolutely vital that the v-shaped incisions into the corners are accurately cut, and that they are deep enough – right up to the corner of the marked stitching lines – otherwise the welt will not turn out flat, but will pull and pucker at the corners. Once correctly positioned, the two short ends of the welt should be sewn (always by hand with a small slipstitch) to the body fabric. Slip the needle between the welt and the body fabric, catching up a small thread from the two separate surfaces each time. In this way, no stitching will show on the surface of the welt (**FIG 16**).

Schiaparelli would take even the simplest and apparently 'untailored' garment, such as a loose smock top, and upgrade it into something totally distinctive by the addition of welt pockets. When you have perfected this technique, try applying them to simple styles, but at unusual angles, for a couture design effect.

FIG 13

FIG 14

FIG 15

FIG 16

Gabrielle Chanel, photographed by Cecil Beaton.

CHAPTER FIVE

Gabrielle Chanel

DRESSMAKER WITH CHIC

Gabrielle Chanel always defied convention, from the moment she decided on a career in fashion. No other female couturier has displayed the determination, originality, and most important of all, the durability that her work embodied. But Chanel is to be remembered not particularly for originality of cut or line, but for her superb workmanship and her innate sense of timing. She responded to changes in women's habits and tastes in a realistic, feminine way which other couturiers could not emulate. She seems to be the ultimate of French womanly chic in her designing.

Her life began simply in a tiny village near Issoire in the French Auvergne, somewhere around the date of 1886 (typically she kept her actual age always a secret). Due to her mother's early death, when Gabrielle was six, she led a lonely childhood in the care of an aged aunt. But her energy, intelligence, and unusual beauty (described by some as *jolie laide*, 'pretty-ugly', though in fact she was much more strikingly attractive than the French words suggest) soon led her out of her limited background. She constantly confused her biographers with apocryphal stories of her life, but it does seem reasonably certain that around the age of 20 she had a job as a nightclub dancer at Pau, in the Pyrenees, where she met a young Englishman, who subsequently set her up in business with a small hat shop in Paris. Situated in the rue Gambon, it was coincidentally only a few doors away from the establishment that was to become her couture house, at number 31.

Even though living and working in Paris, Gabrielle continued her passionate interest in an athletic outdoor life, riding whenever she could. Her early excursions offer one explanation for her famous nickname, Coco: she would get up at the crack of dawn to go for a ride, and was christened 'Mlle Cocorico' (Cockadoodle in French) and the name stuck. Her energy and her wit launched her almost immediately as a success in Paris, for a French magazine shows an example of her millinery as early as 1912, worn by the actress Gabrielle Dorzat.

During the First World War, Chanel moved out of Paris to Deauville, to work for the Red Cross. The next step in her career is so well known that it too seems almost legendary. Based in a little boutique (supplied again by some bewitched lover), Gabrielle watched the war efforts of the wealthy, at this most fashionable seaside town:

One day I put on a man's sweater, just like that, because I was cold. I tied it with a handkerchief at the waist. I was with English people. None of them noticed that I was wearing this sweater. None of them told me it looked good on me, that I looked pretty in it. The English don't tell you anything.

Chanel's own version of the story of course takes a cynical tone, as she so often did, but the effect of her little invention was dramatic. Modelling her own 'creation' with a straight pleated skirt, and topping it with a sailor's pea jacket, she caused a great stir among the war-working ladies of the seaside front. Soon her shop was humming with orders, and her true talent for combining and accessorizing took over. By adding a little brooch, tying the right kind of scarf, sitting up the lapels in a particularly casual but smart fashion, Chanel moved towards her own definable sense of style. As her biographer Marcel Haedrich wrote:

Her stroke of genuis was to transpose the masculine English fashion to the feminine with taste that precluded any ambiguity, as she had already done with hats. She transformed everything she touched – her jackets, her blouses, the ties on the blouses, the cufflinks at the wrists, everything she borrowed from men became ultra feminine through her magic.

After the war, Chanel returned to Paris and opened her salon, this time under the auspices of a wealthy English peer – the Duke of Westminster. They travelled together to the south of France on his boat, and Chanel caused another sensation by appearing at the Carlton Hotel, Cannes, sporting a sun tan – unheard of in polite society in those

An early Chanel design: matching blouses and lapels remained a distinctive feature of her work, Spring 1939.

Her showroom displayed pleated jersey dresses, simple jackets with functioning, not trimming buttons, long evening dresses with bright and original decorations. Her first collection, 1922, showed Balkan embroideries on black crêpe de chine; in 1924, she showed gorgeously drooping chiffon with floating sleeves and long loops of glass and cut steel beads. In 1925 she revolutionized 'separates' with her cardigan jacket two-pieces. In 1926, her straight-hanging jersey dresses epitomized the look of the Jazz Age. Square-necked, or adorned with simple white collars, the bodices hung straight to the hips, modified by careful seaming to give eye interest. From the hips, the dresses would break out in easy pleats as the wearer moved, but the overall silhouette was one of sleekness, an uncluttered elegance. Topped by the ubiquitous cloche hat, it was a look that women of all ages (but particularly young ones) could wear from morning till night. Plain, quite drab colours, beiges, fawns, greys, navys and even black, in spite of recent enforced wartime use of the colour – became ultra smart.

This style of dressing changed hardly at all through Chanel's long career. In the thirties she continued to invent a stream of simply cut, ultimately wearable dresses, and Chanel herself knew exactly how it was that she became so successful. Her very lack of technique and knowledge, at the start, had contributed:

> The dressmakers didn't take me seriously, and they were right. I knew nothing about the business. In the beginning, I had my milliners making my dresses; I didn't know that specialized workers existed. But this was just as well, because I learned everything for myself: I had to know because I had to explain things to my milliners. Besides, it isn't all that complicated. Fashion is like architecture; primarily a question of proportions. The most difficult thing to create is a well-proportioned dress for all women, a dress that five different women could wear without anyone's seeing right away that it's the same thing.

According to her biography, Chanel actually made her dresses on her models, 'cutting the fabric with scissor strokes to make the clothes simpler'. She would often re-design them with pins. Stories from her life reveal a deep and passionate knowledge of fabrics, their feel and movement, and she was a tremendous innovator as is shown by her famous introduction of jersey as a fashion fabric. In 1932 she went to London at the invitation of Messrs Ferguson to promote English cottons, and produced a number of charming 'race gowns' and ball gowns for the débutantes and society ladies of the day. She often had tweeds specially woven for her in Scotland – her simple wool suits, trimmed with braid and lined with silk became famous all over the world and were much copied, later.

Chanel stopped working during the war, and in fact could have continued living in prosperity and seclusion for evermore due to the immense success of her perfume, Chanel No 5, launched in the late twenties to coincide with her entrée into the world of Hollywood as a designer. She did not

days. She also wore artificial jewellery, which, together with her simple jersey dresses, provided exactly the ideal of chic and simplicity desired by women after the war. Prudence Glynn, the fashion journalist, calls it 'functional chic' and comments:

> After the war there was a whole class of *nouveaux pauvres* who needed just such a brilliant idea to restore their superiority of chic. Again it is problematical whether Chanel deliberately set out to fill a void; given her personality it is more likely that she regarded having the real gems given her by her affluent lovers copied in beads as a witty indication from a poor-class girl that she could not be bought by material presents alone.

Possibly true: the English peer, though married, offered to divorce his wife and marry her, but Chanel refused when he made it a condition that she would have to give up her work and live a more suitable life. On the brink of considerable independent success, such an idea was not attractive to her, in spite of the inevitable loneliness which became part of her life. She returned to Paris, to her salon, which by the mid-twenties was the most talked about in Paris.

pick up the challenge until 1954. At first the fashion press resisted her, and a blistering attack was published in the French magazine, *Combat*, containing these malicious words:

Even as usually well-informed sources whispered that she was re-opening her house in order to further the publicity for her perfumes, Chanel was busily denying this, saying that it was only her revulsion at the bad taste of today's Paris dressmakers that had impelled her to emerge from her pleasant retirement. And the eagle eyes of this Cassandra, made new by plastic surgery, were sparkling ... In her games of the future we saw not the future but a disappointing reflection of the past, into which a pretentious little black figure was disappearing with giant steps.

It was a victory for Chanel, to return to complete success and to prove her critics wrong. By the mid-fifties, Chanel-style clothes were firmly established once more as the look of the moment. One English company, Wallis, ran a constant line of ready-to-wear versions of the cardigan suit she perfected throughout the decade.

Chanel suits never varied greatly: in soft, loosely woven tweeds or mohairs, they had linings of silk often in the same fabric as the blouse. Just as before, in the twenties, women had to pay as much for a jersey dress as for one of Poiret's gold-encrusted creations, so it was in the sixties. Courrèges once heard a client complaining that 5000 francs for a Chanel suit, that was after all a mere 'product' rather than high fashion, was too much. He is reputed to have replied (according to Chanel herself):

You're quite wrong to complain about the price of the suit. For 5000 francs I couldn't give you the same thing as Mlle Chanel, who has talent and experience. Next to her I don't exist.

Possibly Chanel was thinking of Courrèges' structured creations when she said:

Men make dresses in which one can't move. They tell you very calmly that dresses aren't made for action. I'm frightened when I hear such things. What will happen when no one thinks as I do anymore?

But many women did think as Chanel did, and when *Elle* magazine ran a Chanel pattern offer in the 1950s they received a quarter of a million requests for it. Then in 1957 she won the Nieman Marcus Award for fashion; in spite of her often harsh words about American 'cheapness' as opposed to 'chic' she found total acceptance there. Chanel herself knew, always, the secret of her success; painstaking workmanship, attention to detail, and above all, relentlessly quiet good taste:

I consider myself quite limited in what I do. Therefore it must be meticulous, and the material must be beautiful. As much as possible I must show a little taste and not change too much. People would say that I was no longer making my clothes.

top *Chanel clothes as they are remembered: a 1962 ensemble, silk blouse, matching lining, gilt jewels.*

above *A simple two-piece that could be worn today. practicality and pure glamour combined, Summer 1938.*

One of the features that distinguish couture-made clothes from ready-to-wear is the way in which linings are mounted into a garment. This is a tradition that is handed down from one tailor to the next, from one generation of couturiers to the next. Even the body section of a Cardin dress, designed along the most 'space age' of principles in the 1960s, was lined throughout in silk crêpe de chine – with the *shiny* side worn next to the skin! There were also pure silk facings to the neck and armhole edges, with the whole garment stitched by hand and even the press-studs at the back of the neck hand-covered with little circles of silk. The dress itself is a mere slip of a mini, made in organdie embroidered with navy flowers.

Among the older generation of couturiers, Chanel stands out as a craftswoman who applied the very highest standards of finish to her clothes. Those neat little suits owe as much to superb tailoring as they do to the talented designing. Every example offers a new special tip that could well enhance another garment. For example, her light mohair suits were fully interlined with silk chiffon, very carefully and lightly mounted to the fabric to give a delicate extra substance. The suit top and skirt were then fully lined (and hand-stitched) with a pure silk lining. An interesting detail seen on a later model (1974) is that Chanel would mount a band of silk, cut on the bias, and hand-stitched, inside the finished waistband of a suit skirt. The suit would, of course, be made with a matching blouse: the silk band inside the skirt would add to the easy ride of the waistband over a tucked-in blouse, and certainly be more comfortable than having the woolly fibres of the mohair fabric, working through the blouse silk to the skin.

The lining of a Chanel suit jacket droops into a soft pleat at the lower back section, in order to hide a heavy gilt chain. This would be hand-stitched to the top of the hem allowance, and completely concealed by the fall of the silk lining, helping to keep the loose-fitting, open-fronted suit jacket in place without riding forward with the wearer's movements. Linings to Chanel's couture clothes usually have tucks in the back, particularly under the shoulder blades. They are used in preference to the darts so often seen in ready-to-wear clothes, which equally often work open due to the stress placed on them while the garment is being worn. On certain bubbly tweed fabrics, Chanel would have the lining lightly mounted to the suit fabric, all over its surface, to give the garment strength and prevent it pulling out of shape.

CUTTING A LINING FOR A JACKET

Linings are usually cut from the same pattern pieces as the garment itself. Make sure to mark all matching notches, and insert all tailor's tacks, especially for the darts and the head of the sleeve. For suit jackets, place the pattern piece 2.5cm (1in) away from the centre fold of the fabric so that a pleat can be made, giving extra ease (FIG 1A, 1B).

Machine stitch the side seams of a hand-mounted lining for a jacket. Stitch the long sleeve seams also and run two rows of small gathering stitches round the sleeve head, in readiness for gathering up the fullness when the lining is mounted in place.

Press in the seam allowances round the front and neck edges of the lining, as a guide for when pinning the lining into place (FIG 2A, 2B).

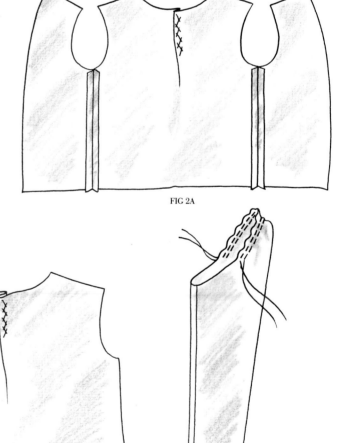

FIG 2A

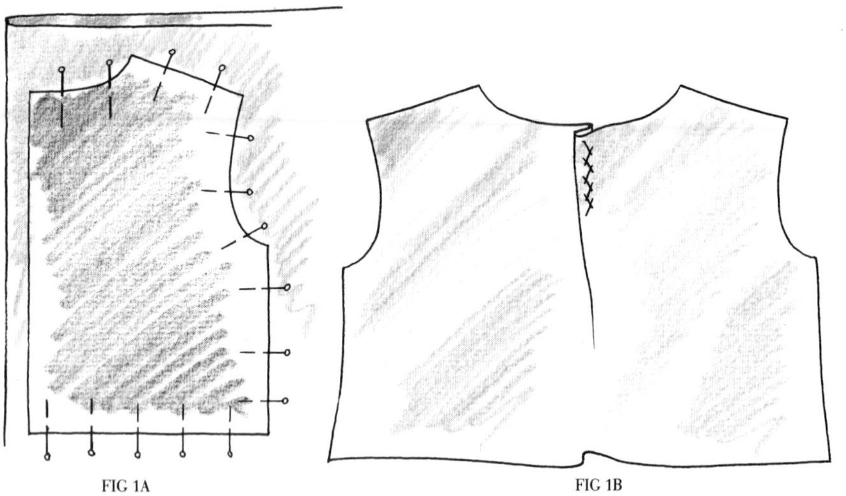

FIG 1A

FIG 1B

FIG 2B

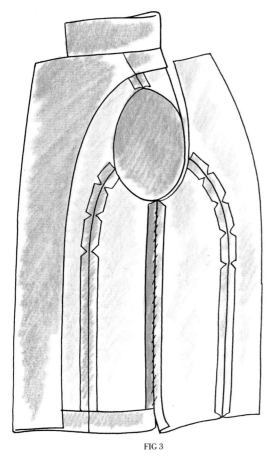

FIG 3

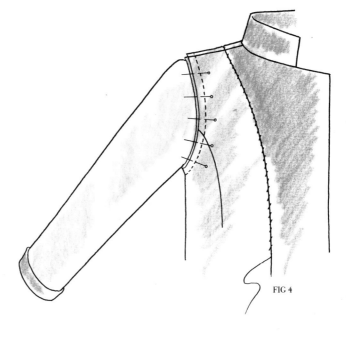

FIG 4

FIG 5

For the tailor method of mounting a lining, a dummy is needed. Failing that, borrow a friend and fit the lining on your own body following their instructions! The made-up jacket itself needs to be turned *inside out*. The joined sections of the body lining are then held up against the jacket, and the side seams are pinned in place first, to make sure that the lining corresponds properly, in position. Pin and tack on the seam allowance, with the front section of the lining flapped back out of the way for the moment. Repeat this step on the other side seam. Make the stitched area about 5cm (2in) short of the underarm, and the same distance short of the bottom edge of the jacket (FIG 3).

Smooth the lining over the two front sections, folding in any dart that may be incorporated in the shoulder line, and tacking it down to a point. Allow for some fullness over the front section of the jacket, for ease of movement. Make the front folded edge of the facing match up neatly with the curving line of the front facing. Pin and then stitch firmly the front section of lining to the shoulder seam allowances, without turning in the fabric – it will be covered by the back lining section (FIG 4).

Work next on the back of the lining: smooth this with the hands up over the shoulder blades, without distorting the lie of the fabric. Make the already-pressed edge of the lining sit on the neck facing, unfolding the edge to make any adjustments necessary. Form the excess fabric into a pleat down the centre back of the lining, and then fold the shoulder edge of the back lining to the exact depth of the seam allowance over the stitched front lining which is already fixed to the seam allowance. Make the stitches as small as possible so that they will disappear into the fabric of the lining. (Leave the bottom edge of the jacket until later, after a final fitting) (FIG 5).

MOUNTING SLEEVES

The tailor method of mounting a sleeve lining is so obvious that it is a wonder that it fell out of fashion with the vogue for machine work. Join the underarm seam in the lining. Run a row of small stitches round the sleeve head, by hand. Turn the stitched sleeve section right side out, and slip it up the finished, reversed jacket sleeve, matching the tailor's tacks at the head of the sleeves. Pull in the gathering threads until the lining sits easily over the shoulder seam. Fold in the edge of the sleeve head and then, working from the underarm upwards to the head, carefully hand-hem the sleeve into position over the body lining. Again leave the bottom cuff edge for final hemming after checking the lining by fitting the garment, right side out, once more (FIG 6A, 6B).

FINISHING LOWER EDGES

It is possible to finish the lower hem, which should be at least 3.75cm (1½in) above the hem of the finished garment, in two ways: it can be stitched by hand and left loose from the jacket itself (this is more common for coat linings) or it can be folded first to 0.5cm (¼in) and then to about 3.75cm (1½in) for a second turning, and finally, lightly slipstitched to the top fold of the garment fabric hem, so that the excess fabric falls down over the fabric hem in a loose fold. The sleeve edges are usually finished in the same way. The advantage of working from the shoulder seams down, following this method, is that a gaping lining is much more easily avoided (FIG 7).

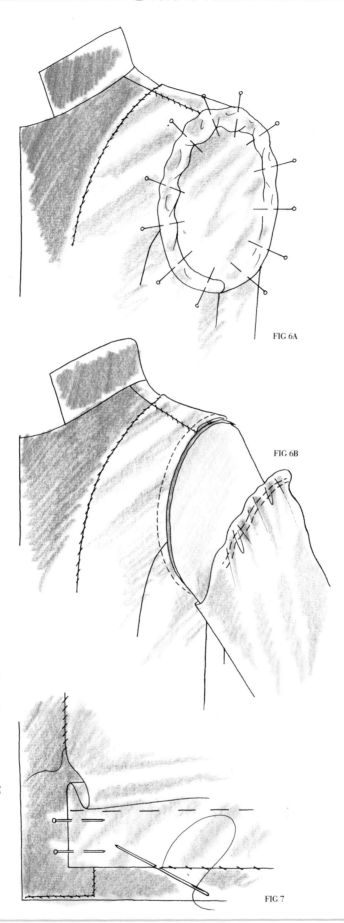

FIG 6A

FIG 6B

FIG 7

DRESS LININGS

Dress linings may be made in one of two ways: in the first, the lining is made up completely, to correspond with the dress itself, except that one seam, either on a shoulder or at the side, is left open. The dress itself is made up, turned wrong side out, and then the lining is slipped over the shape, checked to make sure that all the seams line up and sit without wrinkles or bunches. Finally the open seam is hem-stitched into place, as described for the jacket (FIG 8).

For some dresses, it is sufficient to make a lining that acts as a lining-interfacing, by basting the two layers of fabric together, and seaming them together as one layer of fabric. On very light materials, like those for summer-weight clothes, this is a good method; it eliminates the need for facings, as the dress can merely be trimmed with a bias-cut edging. (A beautiful Poiret dress made in cloth of gold mesh was interlined with gold net, and lined with gold-coloured silk, on this principle: the curved neck and armhole edge were trimmed with piping and covered with a pleated narrow ribbon to complete a very simple but stunning dress, with no bulky facings.) (FIG 9)

SKIRT LININGS

Here is a good method for lining a skirt, somewhat similar in principle to the jacket method, but also adaptable for use with ready-made, unlined skirts.

Always be sure to cut any lining pieces on the same grain as the fabric section it is to back, otherwise the garment will appear distorted when worn. Straight grains have a difference of sit, even between warp and weft, though this is not as pronounced as the difference between straight grain and bias. But it is still enough to spoil a finished effect.

Turn the skirt inside out, lay it front upwards, and place a piece of lining material over the skirt, making sure the grain lines run in the same direction in both pieces of fabric. Pin the lining to the skirt, starting at the *hem* and leaving an allowance for the lining to be finished, at the end of the fitting. Gradually smooth the lining in place up the two side seams of the skirt, as shown for the jacket. Fold in and tack any darts in the skirt lining at the waistband. Once the lining fabric has been fully pinned into place, run basting threads along the seamlines, removing the pins as you work. Then cut out the skirt front section. Repeat this method for the back section of the skirt (**FIG 10**).

Once the skirt pieces have been accurately cut, they can be stitched up by machine separately, and mounted into the skirt at the waistband. Usually skirt lining hems are allowed to hang separately, but the hem must always be adjusted so that it is 5cm (2in) shorter than the hem of the skirt itself (**FIG 11**).

If you are making the skirt completely, as opposed to adding a lining to a ready-made skirt, then the lining can be pinned to the made-up skirt before the waistband is stitched in place. The skirt and the lining then act as one fabric when the waistband is mounted. When making up a skirt, leave the zip placket area open and hand-stitch the lining, with a small turning, to the tape area of the zip once it has been mounted in place.

FIG 8

FIG 9

FIG 10

FIG 11

Post-war elegance: Christian Dior's bustle suit, 1948.

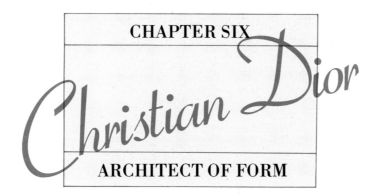

CHAPTER SIX

Christian Dior

ARCHITECT OF FORM

Christian Dior and Balenciaga are the two couturiers who brought the Parisian fashion industry to its highest point of international acclaim. During their years, from the end of World War II until the early sixties, the word of Paris reigned supreme over all fashionable women. People had money to spend in the boom that followed the austerity of the war, and these two men responded to the need for glamorous elaborate clothes, emphasizing the feminine (often at the expense of practicality) but offering a sharpness of style in combination with a dramatic quality that few other couturiers have since achieved.

Christian Dior came from a middle-class background, and spent his youth in comfortable surroundings, first outside Paris, at Granville, and then in the city itself, where he had the money and the leisure to absorb all the exciting new artistic trends of the twenties. As he describes his teenage years in his autobiography, *Christian Dior and I*:

This was the postwar period, a completely new epoch and a fresh start for everyone, including us fifteen year-olds. We were wonderfully in keeping with our times. Officially I was supposed to be studying at the Tannenberg School for my *barichot* examinations but even then, with my friends, I was falling under the influence of music, literature, painting, and all the manifestations of the new trend in the arts . . . As the decade from 1920 to 1930 was a rich one, luxury was shown in subdued materials – reinforced cement, plain wood. In fashion Chañel ordained jerseys, and tweeds; Reboux, untrimmed felt cloche hats. By contrast with the rationalism of the applied arts, the Fine Arts – painting, poetry, and music – became inconsequential. Bonnard, Vuillard, Ravel and Debussy, all seemed too formless and a little out of date; and new gods were Matisse, Picasso, Braque, Stravinsky and Schönberg. The Dada-ists freed language from the tyranny of precise meaning, and shining over every avant garde effort was the blazing light of Jean Cocteau.

Dior's descriptions are revealing: he sets the clothing of the day in the context of other artistic output, and shows how his ears and eyes were constantly stimulated by new sounds, colours, textures; he describes the 'dress' of the buildings, 'reinforced cement, plain wood' in much the same way as he describes the clothes – 'jerseys, and tweeds . . . untrimmed cloche hats'. This understanding of the mood of the time gave Dior an instinctive and sure grasp of what people wanted to wear – and when! Later, when his career blossomed, he was to turn this sensitivity to good use.

In his youth, he amused himself by buying avant garde paintings and running a small gallery off the rue Le Böétie, with a partner, Jacques Bonjeau. But the venture was doomed from the start: it was 1928. A year later, as the Wall Street crash ushered in the Depression, the luxury of the twenties was superseded by the stringency of the thirties. Dior's family was hard hit, and moreover Dior's mother, whom he adored, died in 1930. The family had to sell up everything of value, including their fine antique furniture and valuable paintings; and Christian was forced to look for employment, finally getting some work supplying fashion sketches to magazines in Paris. Thus, at the age of 30, with little formal training, he stumbled into the area of life that was to make him rich and famous – as a fashion designer. His earliest designs were for hats, his dress ideas proving less acceptable at first, but with the sound encouragement and criticism of two well-connected friends, Michel de Brunhoff (who became editor of French *Vogue*) and Georges Geoffrey, a decorator, he was able gradually to improve his portfolio of designs. They gave him advice about colouring, line, and so on; another fashion designer friend, Jean Ozenne, took him into his home and more or less taught him how to sketch. Eventually Dior succeeded in selling some of his work to the house of Robert Piguet, a rising couturier of the time, and by 1938 he was working regularly for him as a designer.

During the war years, Dior spent much of his time out of Paris, first mobilized at Mehun sur Yèvre, and some of the time with his father and sister at Gallian in the southern zone of France. Dior always loved the earth and gardening, a passion which he inherited from his mother. He recalls these years:

> It seems incredible to think that despite my love of art and my many artistic friends, I scarcely knew how to wield a pencil. For two months, I worked night and day at producing ideas and then went back to Paris, my pockets stuffed with designs, determined to win myself a place in the world of fashion.

Dior managed to keep afloat financially by selling the remains of his own collection of paintings, and supplying the Parisian newspaper, *Le Figaro*, with fashion sketches. Eventually he found his way back to the capital, intending to work full-time for Piguet, who had to confess with some embarrassment that he had hired someone else (Antonio de Castillo) instead in his absence! Dior succeeded in finding another position at Lucien Lelong, where he worked alongside Pierre Balmain as co-designer; at that time Lelong did not design himself but ran the business collaboratively with Nadine Cassandre, who later joined Dior in his own enterprise. Another figure at Lelong's who became a crucial confidante and ally was Raymonde Zehnacker; she too was to join the house of Dior.

However, Dior's evident talent was not allowed to go unnoticed for very long. At the end of the war, a friend from Dior's own home of Granville introduced him to Marcel Boussac, head of one of the largest cotton textile companies in France. He was looking for a designer, and suggested Dior work for him. Balmain had by this time left Lelong to set up a house of his own, and Dior felt that everything pointed in this direction for himself too, but he was reluctant to desert Lelong, who had been so kind to him. As a way out of his predicament, Dior lightheartedly challenged Boussac: rather than work for his now languishing house of 'Gaston', restoring it to its former glory, he would only leave Lelong if he could set up a new house, entirely of his own. After a short pause for reflection, Boussac said 'yes' and the Maison Christian Dior came into being. As quoted in *Paris Fashion*, Boussac realized that here was a designer of tremendous calibre, 'a tree to be planted, not just grafted'.

The first showing took place in February 1947, and took Paris by storm with what Dior called 'Corolle', soon to be replaced by the American tag, the 'New Look'. In Dior's own words:

> In December 1946, as a result of wartime uniforms, women still looked and dressed like Amazons. But I designed clothes for flower-like women, clothes with rounded shoulders, full feminine busts, and willowy waists above enormous spreading skirts. Such a fragile air can be achieved only by solid construction. In order to satisfy my love of architecture and clear-out design, I had to employ a technique quite different from the methods then in use. I wanted my dresses to be constructed like buildings, moulded to the curves of the female form, stylizing its shape. I emphasized the width of the hips, and gave the bust its true prominence; and in order to give my models more 'presence' I revived the old tradition of cambric or taffeta linings.

Dior's ideas presented tremendous problems to his cutters and workroom *assistantes*. Technically, no one knew how to put the dresses together at first, and old techniques for handling materials had to be revived. Even the fabrics were 'new' in the sense that wartime scarcity had made them unfamiliar. He learned how to make up his clothes, with their statuesque firmness, underneath, and a soft elegance on the outside, by poring over old fashion plates, and studying old dresses first hand in museums and private collections. One story tells how on a visit to New York, he would disappear for long periods of time into the storage rooms of the collection at the Metropolitan museum, where he would be found enveloped in a Victorian gown, only his legs revealed beneath, staring upwards and busily taking notes about the garment's elaborate construction. On this close study he based a whole collection of cocktail gowns stiffened throughout with cambric interlining.

Dior himself never learnt to sew or even to cut a dress though this last skill has often been the secret of success for many a couturier. Dior's talent lay in finding exactly the right collaborators to execute his designs, and to inspire them fully with the ideal in his head. He would make a series of '*petite gravures*' which he would then hand out to his three key assistants, Mmes Marguerite Caire, Raymonde Zehnacker and Bricard. Where necessary, Dior would give an instruction about the cut of the cloth, the lay of the material, the desired effect to be made. Mme Marguerite would then be responsible for handing the sketches to the appropriate '*premières*' (heads of workrooms), attempting to suit the idea of the dress to the woman concerned. She would be the one responsible for cutting out the muslin model, keeping as closely to the inspiration of the '*petite gravure*' as possible. The showroom *assistantes* sewed up the muslin ready for submission to Dior again. The *toile* would then be subjected to close scrutiny, torn apart, and criss-crossed with French chalk marks to indicate where alterations should be made. For one collection, 60 or more *toiles* would be assembled. As Dior himself revealed:

> Some of the toiles turn out quite different from what I had imagined; they are not necessarily failures, but the design has been misinterpreted in some way. The *premières*, like the photographers and fashion artists, have read into the design something I had not intended.

Interestingly, Dior would often give the same sketch to several different work units within the house, so that he would have a choice of interpretations of cut and line in the *toile* to choose from, selecting the one nearest his original conception.

Every couture collection had to be balanced, to give a representative selection of lines, styles and garments for various functions. Mme Raymonde's job at Dior was to go through the successful *toiles*, and 'map out' a collection, balancing the quantity of dresses with suits, evening gowns, and so on, and giving some working plan for the physical completion of the collection. The choice of model girl for

left *In the fifties a predictable reaction to wartime austerity saw luxurious furs and elaborate trimmings revive in popularity. Dior's 'New Look' emphasized the hourglass figure – some say in sympathy with the overriding social need to boost the birthrate. Whatever the reason, Dior produced a style of clothing that was almost a throwback, in terms of tailoring technique, to the world of Worth.*

above *Christian Dior, sketching. He loved painting and was involved in art dealing before entering the world of fashion. Unlike other couturiers, he was not just an ideas man but became a meticulous craftsman.*

whom the dress was to be made to fit, was also taken into account. In all, Christian Dior would work up about 170 individual 'models' from the basic *toiles* – altering, adding, re-interpreting, and so on. The next step would be to choose the fabric for each of the *toiles* accepted. Many factors had to be taken into account: each model girl had to have a representative and complete range of the collection to display; the colours of the fabric had to suit her personally, but also balance out with the others to be made. (Still today a couturier very seldom actually commissions a fabric from a manufacturer. New ideas in the various textiles are of course submitted to him from the manufacturers practically at development stage, for reactions and suggestions, and notes about colour preferences will obviously filter back to the manufacturer and influence his work. But the couturier is just as likely to be presented with an exquisite finished fabric that immediately inspires him with an idea for a design.)

When the dress had been made up in the actual fabric, Dior would see it again, and make further adjustments to the design on the model:

> This requires a great deal of concentration. A panel worries me; that means its proportions are wrong? Should I make it shorter? No ... it needs lengthening. And the length of the skirt or the sleeves needs to be altered. Then the neckline has to be raised or lowered. Finally the seams fall into their true place. The distance between two of them may need altering by only one fraction of an inch, but it makes all the difference to the success of the model. Placed at a certain point on the body, a seam may produce a broadening effect. With an infinitesimal adjustment, it gives the impression of slimness. All these changes tend toward simplification. Here, a seam is apparently useless, so it is removed; there, some pleats look insignificant; they are replaced by skilful ironing or more cunning use of the fall of the material. For one of the major secrets of dressmaking is that a well-cut dress is the dress which is cut the least.

(Dior's words are exemplified by a black satin evening dress in the Museum of Costume, Bath, the skirt of which has only one seam.) Finally, the dress would be taken away and stitched, to return for vital decisions about buttons, bows, and other trimmings.

Dior was a perfectionist; he spent long hours working on every collection, the only other major interest in his life being the pleasure of his country estate at Coudret, near Milly. He was never a recluse, however, entertaining his friends often and handsomely at his Paris flat, in Passy. Later in his life he bought an estate at Montaurou near Callian, for his retirement.

Every collection after the first and most famous 'New Look' of 1947, succeeded with the public, though often after initial reactions of surprise and resistance. The 'H' line of 1954 and the 'A' and 'Y' lines of 1955 elongated the torso, showing slightly higher hemlines. Also in the mid-fifties, Dior produced some beautiful tunic dresses, excellent examples of his workmanship and superiority in terms of line. His supremacy as Paris's first couturier suddenly ended with his premature death in 1958, slightly more than a decade after his house had opened.

The house of Dior continued to grow as an industry after the master's death, firstly under the brief and mistimed leadership of Yves Saint Laurent, and then under Marc Bohan. Still financed by Boussac, the company diversified into ready-to-wear, perfumes, stockings, jewellery, and became a multi-million dollar concern. As *Paris Fashion* notes: 'the original ten million francs invested by M. Boussac in 1946 were increased to 100 million within three years.'

Christian Dior was the architect of Marcel Boussac's fortune, and in many ways an architect *manqué* himself. While the elaborate style of his clothes is no longer suitable to us today, there are many aspects of his work, small details of technique, which recall some of his excellence. But principally, the great secret of his success was his eye for a line. For ten years after that first stunning collection, all eyes turned to Paris, every spring and autumn, to get the final word on silhouette and (a particular obsession) the length of the hemline. His sense of timing was impeccable: after the war women craved luxury, and Boussac, as one of the leaders of the textile industry, badly needed a boost to trade. Dior was the catalyst, but his clothes became successful primarily because they were extremely flattering; they were glamorous evocations of the mood of the moment, with his talent for creating so many new looks emanating from his great love of shape.

> My real hobby is architecture, which has fascinated me ever since I was a child. Prevented by my family and by circumstances from ever gratifying this passion, I found an outlet for it in dress design. I think of my work as ephemeral architecture, glorifying the proportions of the female body.

left *An evening ensemble, 1954. Dior spent hours in costume museums studying late-19th-century clothes to add to his 'New Look' in structural* *details. Many of his workroom staff had to learn long-lost techniques to produce the effects desired, using traditional fabrics, such as canvas.*

Dior's tailoring methods for his 'New Look' clothes were elaborate in the extreme: in many cases corsets, or rib-cages of fine boning were built into the waist and midriff of a dress, not only to provide the firmness that the silhouette required but, as is the principle of all couture work, so that the boning of the bodice should fit an individual wearer's frame exactly. It ensured that the fullness of the overbodice, deep neckline or draped back would fall with precision.

Each section of pleating would be reinforced with muslin, and the bottom section, over the hem, reinforced with calico, to give an opening sweep to the pleats. One particular trick that Dior applied to many of his dresses was to insert a double fold of fabric (the same as the body cloth of the garment, wool, gaberdine, satin, whatever) and form it into neat pleats, like a fan: this helped the waistline to stand out over the hips without the extra bulk of a full length petticoat. Many of his jackets were completely interfaced with muslin, so that they would have a stiff, sculptured appearance. Pad-stitching the interfacing helped to create curving, stand-away shapes to back lines. Extra fullness at the shoulders would be added by inserting specially-made pads, to the exact proportion required. A grosgrain belt stitched inside the waistband of a Dior dress allowed it to sit firmly into the wearer's natural waistline, while the skirt billowed out, due to the chiffon flounce stitched into the waistband.

Some of the techniques that Dior employed are no longer usable for the kind of soft tailoring that most home dressmakers are likely to attempt today. Though the following notes cover some of his more classic, tailoring details, a quotation from Dior's own writings serves as an inspiration for the kind of intricate care that goes into making a couture suit of the classic formal lines that this couturier perfected – and for some loose-fitting bias-cut clothes. Even made up from shop-bought paper patterns, it offers a trick that may be well worth remembering:

> To facilitate the fittings, the dresses arrive at the studio entirely covered with guide threads. These threads, in contrasting colours that show up clearly against the material, have been sewed through every one of the pieces that make up a dress. One follows the grain of the material, and the other is at right angles to it. The bias lies between the two. The guide threads, pitiless critics, reveal all the possible faults in the cut, and must find points of equilibrum in essential parts of the dress. To achieve the *faux sens* – neither quite on the bias nor quite straight – requires the hand of a master.

From that comment it must be safely assumed that the home dressmaker should concentrate on working with or across the true grain of the fabric, and leave the '*faux sens*' strictly alone!

THE FUNCTION OF TAILORING

All tailored fabrics for suits, coats or dresses are so described because the shaping of the garment is not merely worked into the cloth by the positioning of seams and darts, but also by the very careful manipulation of the fabric, so that shape and curve appears in the body of the fabric as well. It is the difference between a bodice that stands away from the figure with a few screaming angular darts, and one that hugs the rib cage, and swells just where it should round the bust, curving into the armhole or neckline. Tailoring creates soft folds exactly where they are needed, by masses of hand stitching, and pressing, as opposed to ironing: by gentle application of heat, pressure and steam, a good quality cloth can be moulded into a slightly different shape.

INTERFACING

All tailored fabrics would be interfaced in the traditional manner. Interfacing is not to be confused with interlining; this is used to add strength to a fine fabric and is fused to the textile with delicate pad stitching – such as net under lace, or light silk under a particular panel of chiffon. Interfacing is usually made of canvas or calico; nowadays iron-on interfacings are also available, but are not to be recommended because they have nowhere near the give and subtlety of the genuine article.

TYPES OF INTERFACING

WOVEN INTERFACINGS: These are available in all kinds of weights, from almost transparent to thick, canvas-type. Weight is not the only factor: the lightweight interfacings can be soft and pliable, while others can have a stiff, 'crisp' feel to them – often needed for such areas as collars for evening wear. Examples of the lightest fabrics are muslin and organdie, for a soft effect: for a crisper result, stiffened organdies, organza, nylon or marquisette can be used.

For medium weight use (cottons, linens, lighter wools and materials such as denim, flannel, and poplin) there are interfacings to match. For shapes such as tailored sports jackets, and linen suits with specially-shaped jackets, the 'moulding' quality of the interfacing becomes important: how much the interfacing will give into a curve when steam pressure from the iron is applied. Medium-weight canvas, combinations of wool and hair mix, fall into this category. A synthetic such as Terylene will provide a soft-effect interfacing, on the other hand.

For heavy-weight fabrics, such as wools, heavy cottons, brocades, mixes of fabrics such as tweeds or corduroys, canvas wool and hair mixes are also available to give the moulding effect required. Canvases can be found in both 'soft' and 'crisp' varieties.

NON-WOVEN INTERFACINGS: Bonded soft fibres in sheet form are available in natural and synthetic mixes, and unlike some other natural interfacings, they have no shrinkage or dry-cleaning problems. Their added advantage is that there is no grain line, no direction of weave to worry about, allowing small pattern pieces to be cut in any direction on the fabric.

For the dressmaker, the best solution is to buy only from a reputable store where the sales assistants know the qualities of the goods they are selling, and can offer advice.

Very few shops offer such a service these days, but this survey of the fabrics available at least explains the options open to you, so that you know the right questions to ask, and will not buy a fabric that is unsuited to the task.

BASTING

The illustration here shows you how to apply an interfacing to a garment: remember that it will add firmness to the outer fabric, so if you decide to make a jacket and add interfacing, you must use it for each pattern piece, not merely the lapels which would otherwise stand away grossly from the soft body of your garment. As a result, the jacket will be transformed from a flimsy home-made thing into something more durable and better shaped. Suit the technique to the need however, a herringbone tweed would pay for the effort, but a lightweight summer linen might not.

MOUNTING INTERFACING

The interfacing is always cut away from the seam allowance so that there is no bulk in the seams. Remember also that curved seams, such as for a princess-line dress, a waistband, or the cut edge of a neckline, should always be *stay-stitched* first to prevent them stretching out of shape. Do this to the flat pattern pieces before making up and commencing endless fitting sessions: it improves the set of any garment considerably. Tailor baste the trimmed interlining over the area where you want firmness and a gentle curve to appear (FIG 1).

LAPELS

A unique feature of many of Dior's clothes was the soft roll to the lapels: this was achieved by careful hand-stitching to the under layer of the lapel before making up the suit. (In Dior's clothes, as in the work of most of the other couturiers, difficult parts of the work were nearly always done by hand. All the zips seen on his earlier models were inserted in this way with a small and simple backstitch.)

Interface the front area of the under lapel, but cut the piece only up to the foldline of the lapel. Now check with a preliminary fitting on yourself or on a dummy where the roll-line of the lapel will fall. Working 2.5cm (1in) inside this line, stitch a piece of twill tape on the wrong side of the fabric, parallel to the fold line, stretching it slightly to create a little tension. Stitch in place either by zigzag on the machine, or by hand with pad-stitching (this is similar to tailor-basting, but the stitches are much smaller, and the rows more closely positioned). Leave a space of about 2.5cm (1in) at the end of the lapel line, at the jacket centre front opening, to help the lapel to fall back naturally (FIG 1).

Next cut a second piece of interfacing to cover the lapel area, over the tape, and pin further lengths of tape round the edge over the final seamline for the lapel edge. Pad stitch all over this area, making the stitches smaller and smaller as you near the point of the lapel. As you make the stitches, fold the fabric back over your non-stitching hand, so that you set a good curve into the underlapel piece as you work (FIG 2).

None of these stitches, of course, will show when the top side of the lapel is attached in the usual way, but the firmness and curve of the interfaced underpiece will help the lapels to fall back beautifully into place.

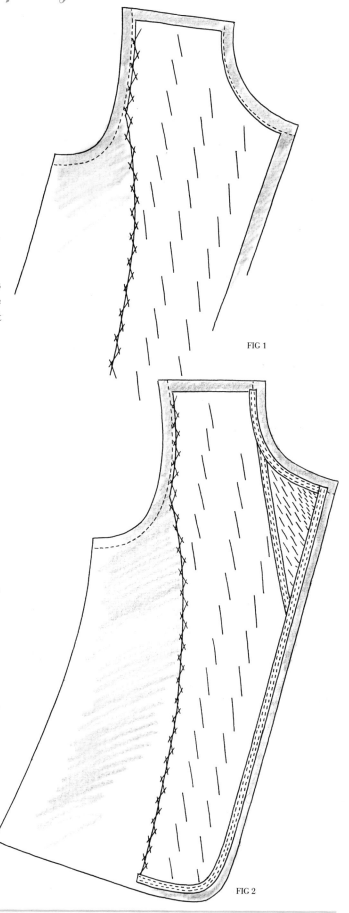

FIG 1

FIG 2

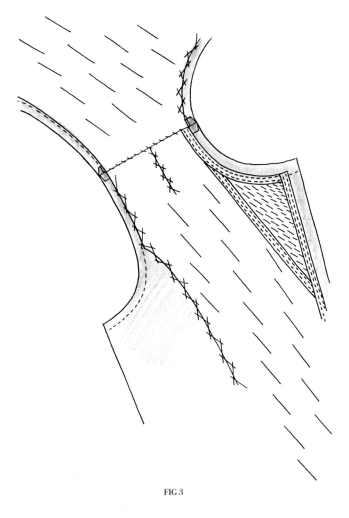

FIG 3

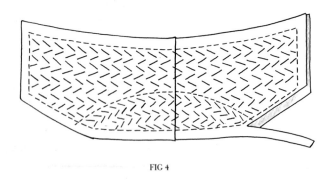

FIG 4

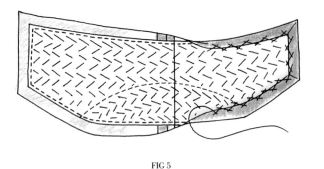

FIG 5

JOINING INTERFACED SECTIONS FOR A LAPELLED JACKET OR COAT

Having interfaced the front section, the back part of the jacket should be treated in the same way. Depending on the stiffness required, the usual area for interfacing is the section over the shoulder blades to give a firm line to the jacket back – no dipping over the shoulder blades. Stitch the interfacing to the back section as described for the front. If there is a centre-back seam, the interfacing is merely lapped over, and stitched through, to avoid bulkiness at the neck edge. The same applies to any neck darts (FIG 3).

Join the shoulder seams of the jacket, taking in only the outer fabric (remember the interfacing is always trimmed away from the seam allowances). Trim and press the seam allowances back flat. Now bring the interfacings over, very slightly overlap them, and catch-stitch down to the seam allowance (FIG 3).

PREPARING AN INTERFACED COLLAR FOR A JACKET OR COAT

Cut both halves of the collar interfacing with the grain in the same direction. Lap the centre-back seam of the interfacing for the collar piece, and stitch through, trimming away any excess fabric. Next place the interfacing on the wrong side of the under-collar piece (which should be cut out in the same grain direction, and joined at the centre). Fold the collar pieces to establish the fold line of the finished collar. Tack, then machine stitch through the interfacing and the fabric along this curving line. Now pad-stitch the undercollar and interfacing, moulding the collar piece in your hands, and attempting to gather in the collar slightly along the curve of the inner neck edge, stretching it slightly on the outer curving edge, so that the collar sits well (FIG 4).

Turn the 'stand' over (following your machine stitching line) and press in order to get a curve into the shape. When the collar is mounted on to the jacket, there should be a continuous and harmonious running line up the front lapel and round this back fold of the collar. Obviously, when the collar is finally mounted, this pressed crease line in the collar will have to be eased out so that the final appearance is one of a soft roll, not a hard line.

Stitch the interfacing, right round the edge of the collar, 2mm (⅛in) inside the actual seam allowance. Now trim away any excess interfacing to just 1mm (1/16 in) inside the seam allowance line. Trim the undercollar fabric to 5mm (¼in), and fold in over the interfacing. Catch-stitch in position, easing the fullness as you go. Shape the collar over the curved cushion (see page 17 for details of equipment), to check how it lies, as before. Check the two halves, folded back to back, to make sure that in stitching and stretching you have not distorted one or other side unevenly (FIG 5).

The next stage is to fit the top collar piece over the undercollar, matching the centre back seams, right sides together, and pin all round. Trim any excess seam allowance away, except round the neck edge. Turn the trimmed edges in so that the fold line extends just slightly beyond the foldline of the undercollar, baste, and then

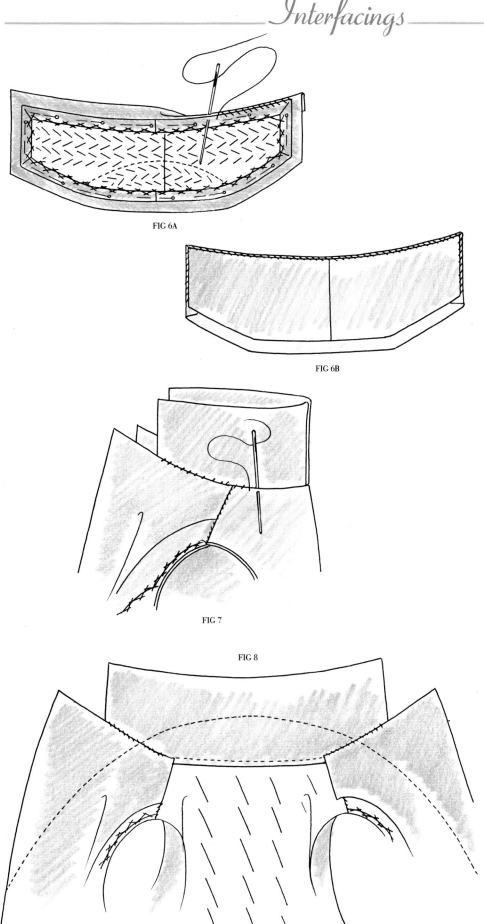

FIG 6A

FIG 6B

FIG 7

FIG 8

hand-stitch the two pieces together, so that the folded edge of the top collar extends just 1mm (1/16 in) over the fold line of the under-collar. This hand work produces a much softer edged, better-curving collar (FIG 6A, 6B).

MOUNTING THE COLLAR TO THE NECK OF THE JACKET OR COAT Place the curved edge of the undercollar right side of fabric against the right side of the jacket-coat. Match the seams at the centre back. Hem-stitch along the seam, through the folded edge of the under-collar taking up the stitches through the jacket fabric and interfacing.

If the collar is in a bulky fabric, clip into the seam allowance of the top-collar, before tacking it down into place on the inside of the neckline. On couture clothes, most of this work is done by hand – even the seam joining the neck facing to the collar will be completed with tiny hand slip-stitches (FIG 7).

Try on the garment, get the collar sitting exactly right, then fold back the seam allowances where the facing and the collar meet, making the collar sit perfectly. Remove the garment, and then slip-stitch this seam by hand. None of this is as time consuming as it might at first appear: with machine stitching, there is always a certain amount of unpicking of uneven stitching to do, or pulling through of the final threads for tying off. You will quickly appreciate that though handwork takes a little longer, it always produces a much softer, neater effect (FIG 8).

Balenciaga's 'ceremonial sheaths' as described by Cecil Beaton.

CHAPTER SEVEN
Cristobal Balenciaga
DESIGNER IN ELEGANCE

Cecil Beaton tells a story that reveals how much eminence Cristobal Balenciaga enjoyed in Paris during his career as couturier, from 1937 to 1968. Nancy Mitford was on her way to the house of Dior, soon after he had opened with such *élan*. The taxi driver (this could only happen in France) turned round and announced proudly, 'At last we have another dressmaker to rival Monsieur Balenciaga!' Until Dior's arrival on the scene, Balenciaga was the most revered and sought-after couturier, for women who wished to dress with a particular severity of elegance, a grandeur that many perhaps would find difficult to carry off. For the exclusive who could, there was no one else to patronize.

His origins were simple: it is known that he was born in 1895 in the small fishing village of Guetaria, in the Basque region of Spain, but more than that has always remained unrevealed. Balenciaga was notoriously secretive, private, and uncooperative with the press, throughout his working life. Legend has it that as a boy he saw a very elegant elderly lady, the Marquesa de Casa Torres walking from church, and had the temerity to ask her if he might copy the dress she was wearing, because it was so beautiful. It happened to be a Paris model, a *tailleur* (tailored suit) in white tussore from the house of Drécoll. The Marquesa was charmed, and obliged; little else is known beyond the fact that by the age of 20 Balenciaga had his own couturier establishment in San Sebastian, and thereafter expanded with houses in Barcelona and Madrid. He was 42 and well-established in his profession, by the time he came to Paris, in 1936 and set up in business with a mere 10,000 pounds capital.

His main reason for leaving, apart from his professional aspirations, was the outbreak of the Spanish Civil War. It seems typical that he should leave the horror in order to continue to do the one thing that he adored, and excelled in. And besides, there were many exiles in Paris, only too ready, in their nostalgia for Spain, to give their support to his new venture. But by the end of the Second World War, Balenciaga had moved well beyond this native circle: he became immensely popular with the Americans returning to

Europe in 1944, and from that time on, his success was assured. Balenciaga continued to remain aloof, private, though never arrogant in his fortune. But he was a source of endless difficulty to the couture establishment and the press. He staged his showings one month after the other Paris houses, to the despair of foreign journalists, who were forced to come back because of his significance. He hardly ever allowed photographs of his collections to be taken, so that a visual record of his work is difficult to find, beyond the few precious examples found in the pages of *Vogue*, each season's exclusives. He was apparently equally firm and severe with his staff, demanding the very highest standards of workmanship and tailoring.

His clothes were predominantly made in his favourite colours, cinnamon, black, brown, sometimes white for contrast, turquoise and often a rich deep red for evening wear – although there are fine examples of bold print dresses that still carry the inimitable mark of distinction that he gave to all his clothes. The Spanish colouring of his models was often noted and he had a demanding eye for colour that would enable him to choose one red out of hundreds, and it would be always exactly the right choice. Carmel Snow (editor of American *Harper's Bazaar*) described his work as 'effortlessly classical', a phrase often quoted because it is the best simple summary possible. He liked formal, sculpted clothes, a lavish use of lace or passementerie, big, bold buttons, and specialized in collars of such curling perfection that they gave the wearer an immediate aristocratic air.

Cecil Beaton, the photographer, said of his work:

His black woollen costumes, ceremonial sheaths of Byzantine embroidery and extravaganzas of jet should be enshrined side by side with the peasant clothes, the sacrificial vestments and ceremonial robes to be found in our national museums, for they form part of contemporary fashion history.

In contrast to his great rival Dior (though there was no personal animosity between them) Balenciaga did not move dramatically from one 'line' to another, from season to

above *An attractive collection of details from the couture collections, including a crêpe blouse, by Balenciaga. His use of bold fabrics was never obvious, sometimes formal, sometimes dramatic, Autumn 1938.*

A characteristic houndstooth wool three-quarters coat, Autumn 1961. The cut, though carefully tailored, brought a new looser line to clothes – the barrel back and easy sleeves are typical of Balenciaga's work, and nowadays seem very modern.

season. His designs evolved more gradually throughout the years of his work. At the same time, many of his designs were so stark and beautiful that they seemed to be years ahead of their time. As *Vogue* put it, in the words of Ailsa Garland, the fashion editor, 1962: 'He has destroyed the time element in fashion. What Balenciaga designed in 1938 looks uncannily right today.'

In general, Balenciaga preferred stiff fabrics to ones that yielded – and as often happens to create success for couturiers, his own inclinations suited a time when the mood was towards grandeur, fullness, formality – a very traditional form of female dressing in general. He is credited with the invention of the use of stiffened fabric to hold out pockets and give a sharp jutting angle to the hips. He also launched mohair as a fashion fabric – introduced by the British firm of Ascher in 1958. What Dior promulgated, Balenciaga refined – where Dior designed, Balenciaga purely tailored. It is said that he would rip a suit apart with his thumbs, remodel and remodel the cloth until he got the effect he required. Beaton comments that it is possible that Balenciaga made few sketches (unlike Dior, for example) and worked more or less according to his inspiration and the fabric.

While appearing to move slowly, many of his lines were forward-looking: beautiful barrel-backed wool coats, three-quarter length, in 1951; loose-fitting suit jackets with box-pleated skirts, the same year; the famous 'sack' shaped dress in 1957, and the distinctive set-away rounded collar (cut out of bias cloth and hand-stitched to the suit jacket) which ran through the collections in the later years, combined with kimono-shaped bracelet-length sleeved jackets. While his clothes are always described as formal, Balenciaga in fact pointed the way to a more easy-to-wear structured simplicity, which his pupil and disciple, Courrèges, went on to develop in the 1960s. It is ironically sad that in 1968 (once again disturbed by political events, this time the Paris students' riots) he suddenly closed down his house, in the belief that the world of high fashion had irrevocably disappeared. He said to Prudence Glynn, then fashion editor of *The Times* in 1972, 'The life which supported couture is finished. Real couture is a luxury which is just impossible to do anymore.' Now the wheel has come full circle: often today's wealthy women look for exactly the quality and workmanship that Balenciaga provided. In an admittedly more muted atmosphere, the present-day couturiers continue their work as always. The style-setting may still come from the streets (perhaps with less surprise to the public than in the sixties and seventies) but individuality and excellence are as much admired as they were in Balenciaga's own era.

In 1973, the Metropolitan Museum in New York staged a major exhibition of Balenciaga's work, 'to honour a giant of haute couture'. Many of the exhibits were landmarks in the history of fashion, like the back-draped overblouse on a bright orange silk day dress (it was later featured in the series, *The Art of Sewing*, Time-Life 1973,) and the extraordinary glamorous balloon-skirted evening robes, in

One of Balenciaga's later designs, with a layered look that also seems still fresh. Unlike Dior, Balenciaga made few sketches, remodelling the materials directly until he got the effect he wanted. He liked to work with stiff fabrics 1952.

heavy, bright-coloured taffetas. Yet it was Balenciaga, who introduced the concept of the body-stocking worn under a loose-fitting overgarment – an innovation much developed after his demise in both couture and ready-to-wear designing.

In complete contrast to the work of many designers who believe that they can transform a woman by bringing out the unseen potential of her body's looks, Balenciaga's philosophy was based on the belief that some women had an indefinable quality of elegance, while others did not. He would use the untranslatable Spanish word, 'cursi' to describe the lack of this quality, and to prove his point would say that two women, wearing exactly the same dress could create quite opposite effects. One would be vulgar, while the other would be distinguished. This attitude may account for the epithets 'daunting' or 'demanding' which are often applied to his work. To define the type of woman he admired, Balenciaga would quote Salvador Dali: 'A distinguished lady always has a disagreeable air'. But then it was always easier to respond to interviews with cryptic remarks. The Marquesa de Casa Torres could not have appeared disagreeable when Balenciaga halted her with the words 'How elegant'; she was undoubtedly beautiful, and dressed with exquisite taste.

Balenciaga was considered to be the finest tailor of Paris. His collars, cuffs and sleeves were immaculately cut and fitted. Of all aspects of the tailor's work, the fitting in of a sleeve head must rank as one of his or her most accomplished tasks, alongside the fitting of a perfect collar. The principle is the same for both: fabric, flat and pliable, has to be moulded into a three-dimensional form, and not a very regular one at that; the 'sit' of a pair of shoulders, and the movement of the arms in their sockets, varies totally from one person to another.

Couturiers stick to certain very simple rules in the construction of their clothes. Basting, for instance, is always worked in one direction, because if you baste up one side and down the other, the fabric tends to twist. This is a particularly valuable detail to remember when tacking up a sleeve. In the classic days of tailoring, using the heavyweight wools and tweeds that Balenciaga favoured, a great deal of work went into the construction of the sleeve before it was attached to the sleeve head. Couture coats and suit jackets often have an apparently unnecessary panel effect on the inner arms as the sleeve is made of two pieces of fabric, not

one. This device was used in order to incorporate a slight curve into the tubular nature of the sleeve, by stretching the outer sleeve, and shrinking in the narrow 'under sleeve' section, so that the sleeve hangs with a forward curve and makes movement that much easier.

Another very common mistake made by amateur dressmakers is to make corrections to the fitting of a sleeve or neck by cutting into the armhole or the neck hole, in order to alter the shape of the sleeve hole or neckline. The top corners of the pattern, at the neck and at the sleeve head, should not be tampered with: the correct points for making alterations are in the dart at the centre of the shoulder line, at the back of the neck, or in the dart over the bustline. They may seem unrelated, but a judicious adjustment or easing of fullness in these places will result in a better sitting (and fitting) sleeve hole. The same applies to the sleeve itself: it is a mistake to cut away fabric from the top of the sleeve head in order to alter the shape of the sleeve. This will only reduce the volume of the sleeve at the top of the arm, and shoulder head, and distort it completely.

To FIT A TAILORED SET-IN SLEEVE

Mark the top centre point of the sleeve head with tailor's tacking. Then make two lines of small running stitches by hand or by machine, round the head of the sleeve, on the seam allowance, as shown. Use the notches marked on the pattern, if you are using a commercial one. Pin, baste, then join the underarm seam in the usual way, and press the seam allowances flat open (FIG 1).

Turn the sleeve out to the right side and, working on the *right* side of the garment, pin the underarm section of the sleeve into place (i.e. the ungathered area of your sleeve). Baste this section of the sleeve firmly (FIG 2).

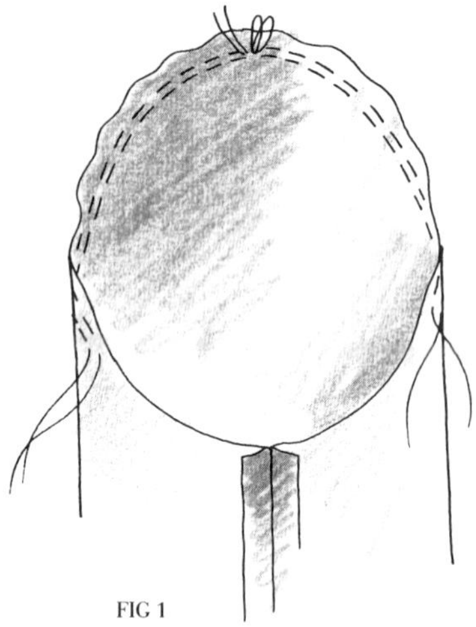

FIG 1

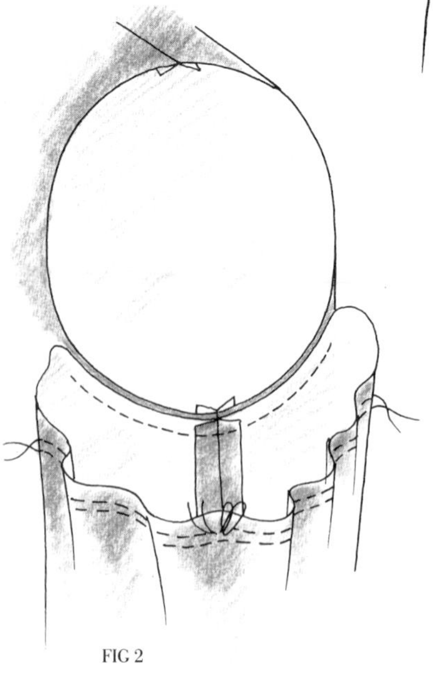

FIG 2

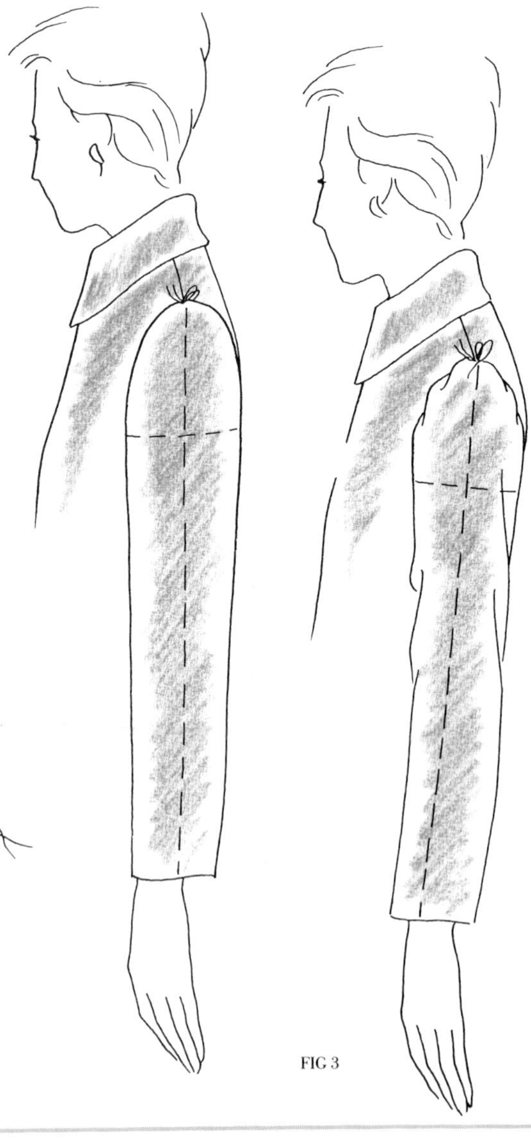

FIG 3

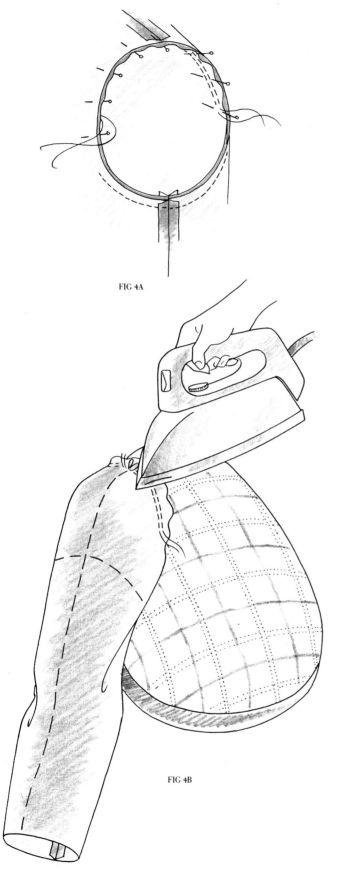

FIG 4A

FIG 4B

Now turn the garment inside out, and pull the sleeve up, easing it up into the top shoulder area of the armhole. Slightly gather up the threads in the sleeve head, until the sleeve fits the armhole exactly. Try to avoid gathers falling exactly on the shoulder seam, and either side for 1cm (½in). Pin and then baste the sleeve into position. Check, as in the diagram, that the sleeve is hanging completely true from the top of the shoulder. (A useful guide is to run basting stitches up the length of the sleeve, and across the centre part of the arm, while it is a flat piece, so that you can check that the sleeve is hanging correctly, once it is made up.)

The set of a sleeve will soon become apparent when you try on the garment, and move your arms slightly. Take a few stitches with the ends of the gathering threads, to fix the fullness required (FIG 3).

Once the sleeve has been correctly basted into position, unpick the sleeve, and then steam press the gathered area, using only the tip of the iron. Keep the heat as much as possible on the seam allowance area, and not on the sleeve head itself, which might cause it to stretch and bulge. Use a sleeve roll to do this. In good quality wool fabrics, the gentle gathering will quite perceptibly shrink back, so that the finished sleeve head fits smoothly, without a wrinkle, while incorporating into the structure the maximum amount of 'give' for the wearer's shoulder and arm (FIG 4A, 4B).

Once the sleeve has been shrunk in this way, the sleeve can be re-positioned, basted and stitched in place. Using the machine, it is always best to make the seam in one continuous thread, starting at the underarm seam, and working round again. Then reinforce the underarm area with a second row of stitching, as illustrated. The seam allowances should be pressed into the sleeve head, to provide support for the sleeve (FIG 5).

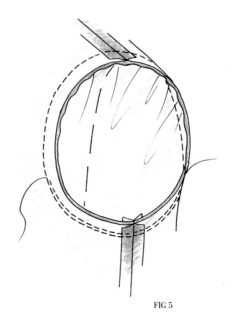

FIG 5

SHOULDER PADS

Balenciaga often created the fullness he required in a sleeve head by the cut of the shoulder top and the sleeve head, with no extra internal support. But the style of the fifties often called for the insertion of more defining pads. Sometimes commercial patterns do not specify the use of a shoulder pad, and it may seem a laborious addition to a coat or jacket, particularly nowadays when styles are much softer than in the hey-day of formal tailoring. However, even a modest shoulder pad can help to correct a figure fault – shoulders that slope, too narrow lines, or an uneven set to the shoulders. Couture clothes like Balenciaga's often have slightly different sized pads inside for just this purpose.

You can make your own shoulder pads from readily-available synthetic padding fabric, following the shape outlines in the diagram. Ready-made pads are available, if all that is required is to accentuate a line, but these of course will be less helpful for figure corrections. A set-in sleeve, like the one described, should have a straight edge, which will overlap the armhole by just 9mm (⅜in). Obviously, a raglan sleeve or dropped shoulder line needs a pad with a rounded shape, as there is no seam to camouflage it (FIG 6A, 6B, 6C).

Shoulder pads should always be lightly basted into position for the fitting of the garment, and most carefully slip-stitched into place, also by hand, as the stitches will give the flexibility needed. Attach the pad to the seam allowance of the shoulder line and round the seam allowance of the armhole, as shown. Sometimes, a sleeve head can also be supported (with or without a shoulder pad), by using a small piece of fleece, or even the same fabric of the garment, if it is the required strength.

Fold the oblong of fabric (size will depend on the shape of armhole) so that one edge is one-third inside the other, and slip-stitch the folded edge of the armhole seam. (Some of Balenciaga's evening gowns, made in satin, often have a folded, pleated slip of fabric inserted into the sleeve head, in this way, to add fullness to the shoulder top line.) (FIG 7A, 7B)

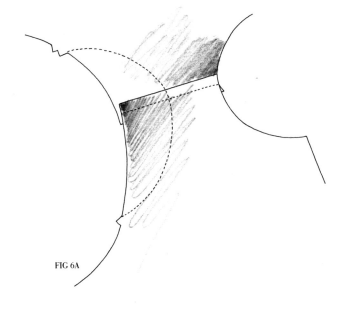

FIG 6A

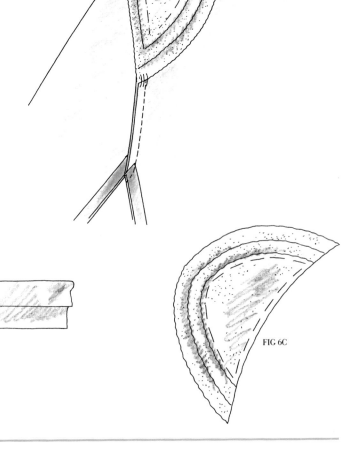

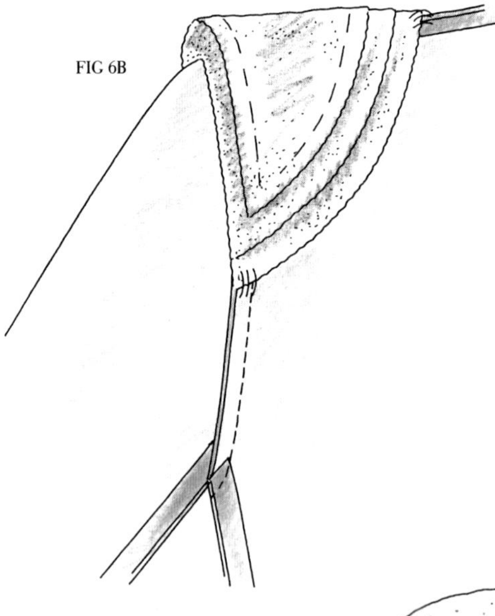

FIG 6B

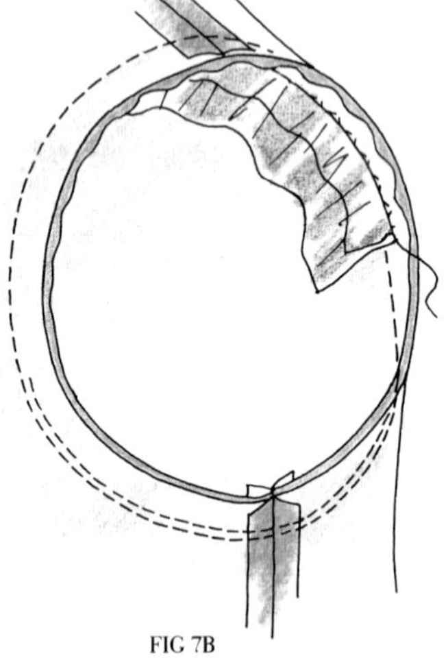

FIG 7A

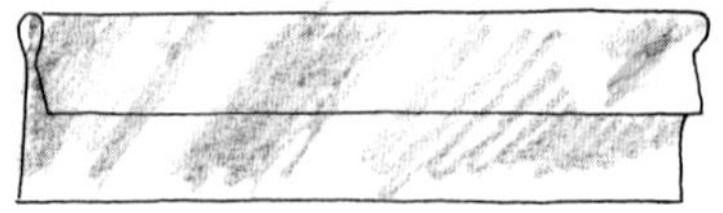

FIG 7B

FIG 6C

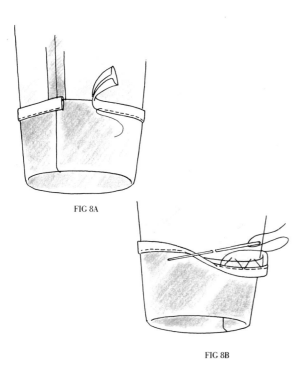

FIG 8A

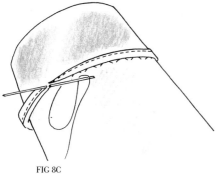

FIG 8B

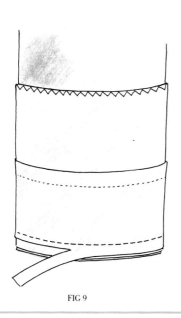

FIG 8C

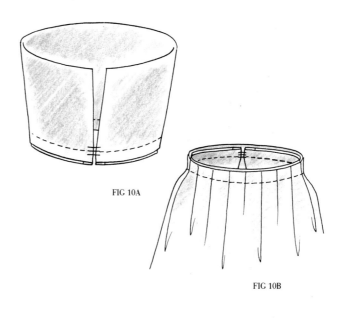

FIG 9

FIG 10A

FIG 10B

To FINISH THE ENDS OF SLEEVES

Couture sleeves are usually bound with bias-cut lightweight lining fabric, mounted on the right side of the sleeve end, and then folded over the cut edge. The edge is then slip-stitched through, from the front of the bias strip, to catch the back fold into place, just below the original stitching line (as illustrated). This neatened edge is pinned in place, to the correct depth of the sleeve. Slip stitches are inserted between the lining strip and the sleeve fabric to catch the sleeve end in place (FIG 8A, 8B, 8C).

Alternatively, a cuff can be added to a tailored sleeve. In construction, the cuff is made in the same way as a tailored collar, with the under-cuff interfaced to give it extra body and crispness. When mounting a cuff, it is wise to grade the seam allowances, so as to avoid bulk when the cuff is mounted.

Most examples of Balenciaga's couture designs have the sleeve cut to exactly the required length, with a separate cuff stitched on to the end of the sleeve. (FIG 9).

A useful tip when mounting an open cuff to a closed sleeve is to hand-baste the prepared cuff together at the seamline; this will prevent it spreading during stitching. And if the sleeve end is to be gathered into the cuff, work with the gathers to the outside of the cuff piece, not the other way round, as it is easier to adjust the gathers evenly in this way (FIG 10A, 10B).

A couturier like Balenciaga would prefer not to use hooks to fasten a sleeve, because they can so easily catch in the material and wear holes. Likewise, press studs were always avoided, as they are strong enough to tear the material. Buttons and loops were considered preferable, and still are best for a fine finish.

American fashion at its best: a Claire McCardell dress, Summer 1949.

CHAPTER EIGHT

Claire McCardell

INNOVATOR OF SIMPLICITY

No couturier is a better inspiration for the fashion student or home dressmaker than Claire McCardell, the most unusual and distinguished of American designers. Not a couturier, in the sense of designing clothes for individual, private customers, she was nevertheless, a top designer, an innovative force in American fashion for years, ahead of her time, and justifiably the winner of the American Fashion Critic's Award, the Mademoiselle Merit Award, and the Nieman Marcus Fashion Award (like Christian Dior before her). Many of her designs are so basic, simple, and advanced that they could be worn today: a brief survey of her work will inspire the creative talent of any individual.

Claire McCardell was born in Frederick, Maryland, in 1905, to a wealthy banking family, and studied at the Parson School of Design in New York – the nearest her professionally orientated family would allow her to get to her passion for designing and making clothes. She maintained her enthusiasm, however, by part-time work at an amateur theatrical club run by students, where clothes from the old wealthy lady patrons would be handed on for making up costumes. Some were model gowns from Paris, and Claire enjoyed many hours unpicking and studying these remnants of foreign glories. Many dresses were refitted and worn by the students – not as costumes but as finery.

Part of Claire's studies included a year's course in Paris, which she undertook in 1926. Not surprisingly, the work of Vionnet in particular, and of the current darling of high society, Chanel, made the greatest impact on her. On returning to New York, and completing her studies, she found her first serious employment with a knitwear company, Sol Pollack, and while the venture was not entirely successful (Claire's ideas being as yet unsuitable for a mass ready-to-wear organization) it did help her to get established in the American fashion industry. After a short stay, she was introduced, by an old school friend, Gay Roddy, to Robert Turk, of Townley Frocks, and secured a job as his design

assistant. In 1931, Turk was accidentally drowned, and McCardell found herself put in charge of design at Townley – a job she was to execute with admirable skill for seven years.

As with the French couturiers, Claire McCardell's success lay in her sensitivity to changing needs. This was the time when American fashions were dominated by the French look, heavily padded shoulders to suits, elaborately decorated dresses, and complex seaming. Her first innovation was a series of 'separates': jersey tops and skirts in black jersey. Culottes, long or short skirts, could combine with halter-necked tops, while a jacket served for day or evening wear. The concept was revolutionary, totally American, and at once successful. It is true (and Claire herself said she did what everyone else did at the time, copy Paris) that jersey had been introduced by Chanel some time before, and that sporty separates were very much admired in Europe, but the idea of a co-ordinating wardrobe, offering endless computations, was different, practical, and economical. While removed from the working atmosphere of couture, Claire McCardell proved herself from the start to be a designer of originality.

She claimed that all her designs came from clothes ideas she needed for herself: 'It just turned out that other people need them too'. After a transatlantic crossing, during which she suffered intense cold in one of her lightweight French wraps, she ended up designing one in tweed. After ski-ing, and noting how cold her ears became, she designed a sports jumper with a hood. And European travel, old-style, accompanied by several trunks and suitcases, was apparently the motivating force behind the creation of the separates collection, mentioned above.

Her next major success came in 1938 with an equally innovative dress, known as the 'Monastic', which was a bias-cut, tent-like garment. It appeared shapeless, but due to the cross-cutting, it moulded itself to a woman's figure in a becoming way. The Monastic was in a direct line of descent from the bias-cut dresses of Vionnet, which McCardell had admired so much in Paris. A reluctant buyer from Best and Company, a major New York store, took an order, and within days found himself inundated with demands for the dress. Unfortunately, the director of Townley Frocks, Henry Geiss, was unable to make best use of the tremendous advantage his designer had given him. The dress was pirated by hundreds of ready-to-wear manufacturers, and eventually forced the closure of the firm.

Claire then moved to the well-known firm of Hattie Carnegie – the nearest she ever came to a couture-type operation. The collaboration was not entirely successful, Carnegie's clientele finding the clothes too 'simple' to justify the prices they were expected to pay (a reaction that would cause horror in French houses). But a new life for McCardell came from an unanticipated source: her old employer at Townley, Henry Geiss, came to her with a new partner, Adolph Klein. Townley was reopened with Claire McCardell featured as the label's designer: 'Claire McCardell Clothes by Townley'. In a short space of time, the clothes, in soft jerseys, rayons, calicos and denims, were selling successfully in New York's most selected store, Lord and Taylor. Sally Kirkland, McCardell's biographer in *American Fashion*, comments on these early designs, christened the first 'American Look' clothes:

> Understandably, its fans are apt to get a bit testy when "the Typical '40s Look" is revived by young designers (including St. Laurent) who have done their research by watching World War II movies on the "Late, Late Show". *Their* forties girls have padded shoulders, padded bras, and high, high heels. Claire's girls were padless, braless, and heel-less. *Their* girls are tightly encased in sexy rhinestone-trimmed satins for big dates; Claire's casual jersey dress-up clothes were more subtly sexy ...

Claire McCardell's clothes were successful because they were, first and foremost, comfortable and easy to wear. Looking at examples of her forties designs, it is impossible to see anything dated or ageing in the designs: they are minimal, simple, and rely on totally functional decorations for their effect: a drawstring made of rouleau, a coat with deep-puffed sleeves so that it could be worn over a plain day dress, or a more elaborate evening frock; trousers with generous pleating at the waist, and a never-shifting tabbed belt; or all-in-one dungaree type outfits, suitably loose-sleeved and collarless, avoiding tailoring details that would make them obviously borrowed from male wardrobe. (The rouleau drawstring of course was borrowed from her French original: Vionnet, and the Greek influence is apparent in the movable, detachable twists of these long round cords in McCardell designs.)

Polaire Weissman, former curator of the Metropolitan Museum's Costume Institute suggested that Claire used old costume books, museum examples, besides the exigencies of modern travel, as sources for her ideas – almost any source

above Claire McCardell made easily worn but very elegant clothes in soft, untailored styles like this jersey dress, 1950. Rouleau and other emphasizing belts were a favourite.

right One of the first to use synthetics, Claire helped to give the fabrics status in the post-war years. Rouleau trim is used again, a style reminiscent of Vionnet.

provided inspiration, from the Edwardian era to Western mail-order clothes – but most particularly early eighteenth century children's clothes, and recalls in *American Fashion*:

> The collarless neck and drawstring back of a little girl's party outfit turned up in one of Claire's best coats. A Dutch boy's full fold-over trousers were the inspiration for an excellent wrapped-front skirt. An elegant Edwardian lace-trimmed diaper cover metamorphosed into one of Claire's famous jersey bathing suits of the 1940s.

Like all couturiers and designers, Claire had a particular sensitivity about fabrics. While she did not work with luxury brocades and rare items like her French counterparts, she did match them in the originality of her use of materials. American cotton had always been seen as a highly practical textile: in Edwardian days ladies would buy 'Tub dresses' by mail order catalogue and launder them relentlessly at home. Claire used very fine voiles to make extremely glamorous halter-neck evening dresses, transforming women's appreciation of fabric conventions at the time. In her first Townley

collection, the 'Kitchen dinner dress' made its appearance – again, a very American notion. It was a pretty, cotton, long-skirted dress, that could be washed at home, but was still attractive enough to entertain in. The style was often made with a matching apron. Calicos, seersuckers, ginghams and denim were other traditional American favourites which were re-considered in her inspired designs. Her innovations continued with the early synthetics, such as Nylon and Dacron. Throughout the 1940s, Claire McCardell produced a number of original ideas but perhaps the most enduring success was the 'Popover' dress, first seen in 1942, which originated as a housewife's 'wrap' dress. Apparently, within its first year, the Popover sold more than 75,000 times. Its shape was to be repeated and refined over the next years, in keeping with its immense popularity.

Sports and playclothes of various kinds were another noteworthy feature of Claire's work: the curious 'Diaper' bathing suits, deep V-necked jersey one-piece costumes, and winter-weight separates, based on matching tights and jumpers, or leotards as fashionwear, were among other McCardell originals. Her use of bold prints, abstract designs, prefigured the work of Parisian designers two decades later – significantly, Emilio Pucci, the Italian who produced such sizzling-coloured leisure wear himself, rated her the best designer America produced. As a demonstration of her modernity, a major retrospective exhibition of her work was staged in her honour, in 1972. Fourteen years after her death, the clothes were greeted with admiration and applause. They were as original, fresh, and easy to wear as when they made their first appearance.

Claire McCardell's career, expanding steadily throughout the forties and fifties, ended abruptly in 1958 when she died of cancer. But the practicality of her clothes still stands as an outstanding example to other designers: fashion need not be exclusively priced to be top-quality in concept. Claire believed that women should look as individual, as easy as possible in their clothes – her styles, albeit simple, are capable of looking entirely different on various women, and yet flatter them all. She once said: 'Clothes make the woman, but the woman can also make the clothes. When a dress runs away with the woman, it's a horror'. One of her leading customers, Stanley Marcus, said of her: 'She is the master of line, never the slave of the sequin. She is one of the few creative designers this country has ever produced'. Although he made the remark in 1955, for a cover story printed in *Time* magazine, Claire McCardell has not slipped from her position of eminence in the succeeding years, but rather, in retrospect, consolidated her achievement.

It is no coincidence that all the women featured in these profiles of the couturiers have injected a strong note of practical innovation in their designs. There is an appreciable difference of approach between male and female designers. Claire McCardell ranks with Vionnet and Chanel as an abundantly realistic rather than fantasy-fulfilling, dress-maker.

left *The famous 'bubble' swimsuit in calico that was intended to be worn belted or unbelted. Claire's innovations in leisure wear were as notable as her daywear ideas. They seemed obvious but were, in fact, completely new.*

above *Claire McCardell wore this sheath dress to receive her award from President Truman for outstanding achievement, 1950. The permanent pleating is characteristic of her modernity; while the shaping remains classic.*

Though not herself a couturier, Claire McCardell's designs were of such quality that they offer many useful new ideas to the designer and the home dressmaker. Her trimmings were simple and effective: she loved big patch pockets, rouleau belts and buttonings, all manner of bold belt details, and gave the new synthetic fabrics a classy look that they had not enjoyed before. Here some of her details are outlined so that they can be incorporated into the simplest of pattern shapes.

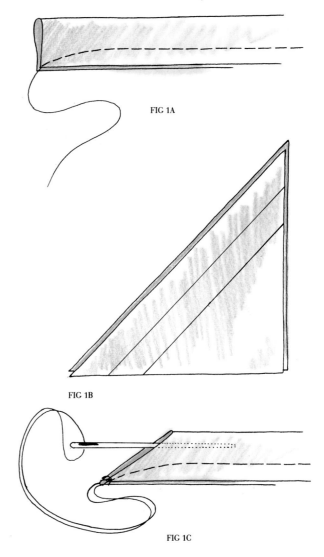

FIG 1A

FIG 1B

FIG 1C

WORKING WITH KNIT FABRICS

First, some advice about working with knit fabrics. These are notoriously difficult to fit well, and cheap examples have very little give and moulding quality. They should be avoided. If you do decide to use a soft jersey, avoid a design that calls for the use of bias in the shaping. The 'give' in a knit fabric is in the grain, and if used wrongly will merely produce a shapeless, lumpy outfit. Skirts with a flare or cut on the cross should be discounted. On the other hand, draped shapes, such as batwing sleeves or cowl-hooded tops, look excellent in these soft-moulding fabrics. When sewing with lightweight jersey, there is a tendency for the edges of the fabric to roll back on themselves during cutting and handling. This can be avoided by basting tissue paper to each layer (a technique often used for lightweight fabrics such as chiffons and satins also): leave the tissue paper attached to the fabric when pinning and basting the pieces together, machine-stitch through the tissue, and then tear it away when the seams are completed.

For the perfectionist, it is often worthwhile using a pattern that has been well-fitted beforehand, or made up in a trial toile; this will avoid unnecessary stretching and distortion of the fabric edges during handling. An alternative technique to prevent seams from puckering or bagging during making up is to stay-stitch the edges of all seam areas before making up. This will ensure that the jersey does not pull out of shape during construction.

Many patterns suggest the use of a zigzag seam for making up jersey – this works well for loose-fitting shapes, but will not give a perfectly-defined seamline on completion. Stay-stitching, careful hand-basting, and straight stitching, using a slightly loose tension, works well instead. If the seam allowances curl, try making a second row of machine-stitching on the allowance, about 0.5cm (¼in) away from the joining seam, and trimming the seam allowance back to this edge. The seam will then lie flat more successfully. On seams which will undergo strain, such as shoulder seams, a piece of pre-stretched tape can be basted into the seam line and stitched into the joining seam, to prevent the stitching breaking open.

ROULEAU FOR BELTS AND FOR LOOPED BUTTONHOLES

Rouleau is rounded cord, often found on McCardell dresses for decorating a surface, making a belt, or forming looped buttonholes. The essential is that the bias strips should be cut four to six times wider than the thickness of the tube required so that the spare fabric forms the 'filling' for the rouleau. A useful guide is to make the stitching seam about 6mm (¼in) from the fold for average-weight fabrics, and 3mm (⅛in) on finer surfaces. Remember that any joining seams you make in bias-cut strips must always be made on the straight grain of the fabric.

BASIC ROULEAU: Fold the strip of bias-cut fabric in half lengthways, right side out, press in place and then stitch the required width from the fold. Take the final stitches at each end, down from the seamline to the cut edges. Use the cut ends to thread through a bodkin, and turn this back through the tube, pulling the fabric over on itself (FIG 1A, 1B, 1C).

CORDED ROULEAU: Cut a strip of cord twice the length required for the finished piece. Fold the bias fabric over the cord, right side out, and baste, then machine-stitch using a zipper or piping foot. At the centre, stitch over the end of the fabric piece, attaching it firmly to the cord. Working from the other end, fold the fabric back over the cord, and work until it reverses, right side out, over the other half of the length of cord. Cut the extra piece of cord away. (If you use a soft, cotton cord (pre-shrunk) this method is very suitable for belts, which have to have a certain firmness in order to keep their shape.) (FIG 2)

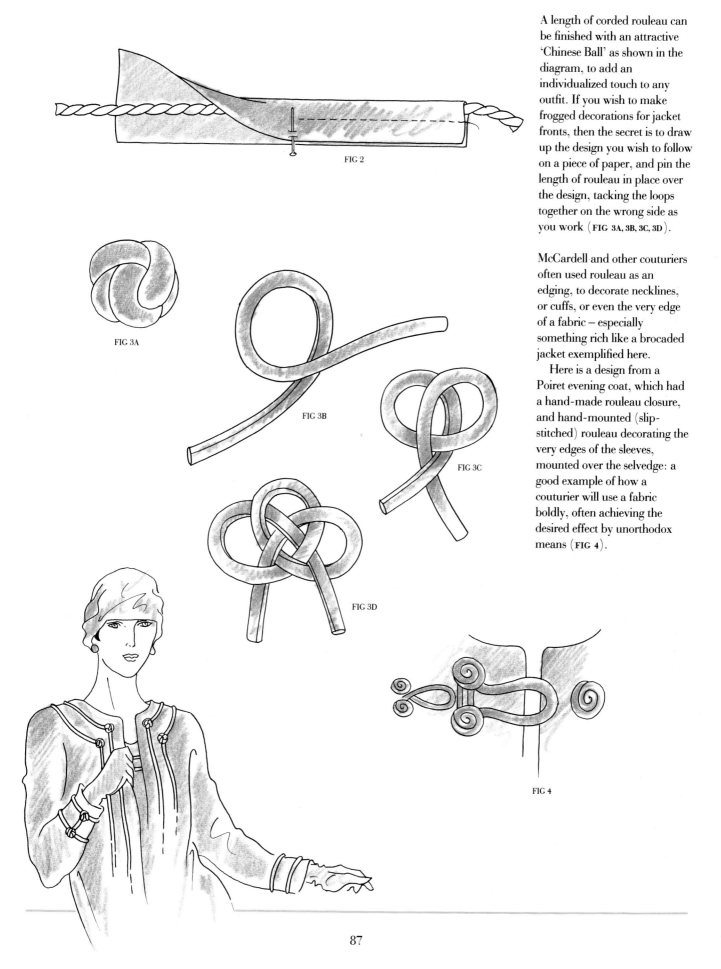

A length of corded rouleau can be finished with an attractive 'Chinese Ball' as shown in the diagram, to add an individualized touch to any outfit. If you wish to make frogged decorations for jacket fronts, then the secret is to draw up the design you wish to follow on a piece of paper, and pin the length of rouleau in place over the design, tacking the loops together on the wrong side as you work (FIG 3A, 3B, 3C, 3D).

McCardell and other couturiers often used rouleau as an edging, to decorate necklines, or cuffs, or even the very edge of a fabric – especially something rich like a brocaded jacket exemplified here.

Here is a design from a Poiret evening coat, which had a hand-made rouleau closure, and hand-mounted (slip-stitched) rouleau decorating the very edges of the sleeves, mounted over the selvedge: a good example of how a couturier will use a fabric boldly, often achieving the desired effect by unorthodox means (FIG 4).

FIG 2

FIG 3A

FIG 3B

FIG 3C

FIG 3D

FIG 4

PATCH POCKETS

A McCardell detail that makes an enormous difference to the look of even the most casual garment, is the making and mounting of patch pockets. These can be made unlined, of course, but the best and most durable finish is not only to make the pockets with a hand-mounted lining, but to position the pockets on the garment while it is being fitted on the figure – or at least on a tailor's dummy – so that the 'sit' of the pocket conforms to the curve of the area where it is in place. So often, pockets look stuck on and ill-fitting, simply because this detail has been neglected.

Cut the pocket pieces and then, if the fabric needs backing and stiffening, cut matching interfacing sections. Baste the interfacing (see page 68) and trim off the seam allowances (also trim away the area at the top where a fold-back is required). Fold the seam allowance of the pocket fabric over the interfacing. Notch into the corners several times, very carefully, and run a tiny gathering thread, close to the folding line of the seam allowance, so that you can gather up the surplus fabric at

the pocket corners, and make the seam allowance sit flat. (For square corners, follow the diagram for a less-bulky method of corner-making.) (FIG 5A, 5B)

Cut out the lining fabric to match the pocket pieces. (The top edge will require only sufficient for a single turning under the top fold of the pocket itself: cut away any extra.) Next turn in all seam allowances, following the procedure just described for the pocket itself. Place the lining, wrong sides together, on the pocket, and pin in place. Hem-stitch carefully round the edge, keeping the lining just inside the turned back allowance of the pocket. Once completed, fold down the top edge section of the pocket, over the lining, take one narrow turning, and slip-stitch the top turning to the lining, as shown (FIG 6).

The pocket should now be fitted on the garment, its position and curve corrected. Couture patch pockets are usually slip-stitched, by hand into place, to allow for maximum flexibility. Top-stitching (see page 94) can be applied before mounting for a decorative finish.

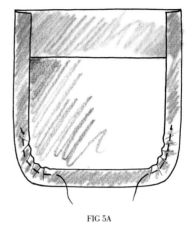

FIG 5A

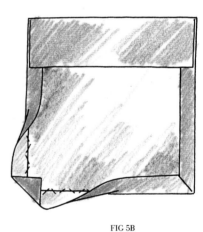

FIG 5B

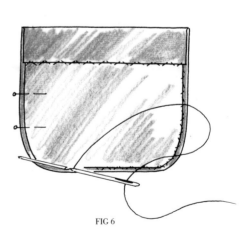

FIG 6

IN-SEAM POCKETS

On couture clothes, a detail that is often missing from ready-made garments is that the pocket underside section is often cut in one with the body of the dress or skirt (obviously a very luxurious use of fabric). If the fabric is light enough, the same will apply to the top inside of the pocket also: alternatively, you could at least cut the underside with the actual dress or skirt section, and only the topside with a matching lining. The final effect is not only smarter, but obviously sits better, with no bulky extra seam on the hip line.

If you do decide to cut the pocket sections separately, it is worth reinforcing the seam with a piece of lightweight tape, as illustrated, to prevent the seam from pulling out of shape or breaking the stitching, once in use (FIG 7A, 7B).

BUTTON LOOPS

An extra feature, related to rouleau, is to avoid button holes by using rouleau loops. These can be made continuously, as shown, stitched between a garment edge and a mounted facing. Rouleau can be inserted into a cuff in the same way. You can also form loops on a folded edge by merely stitching finely to join the rouleau at regular intervals (FIG 8A, 8B, 8C).

Rouleau, or bought cording, can be used in place of piping round the edge of pockets, or even over seamlines as decoration. Slip stitch in place.

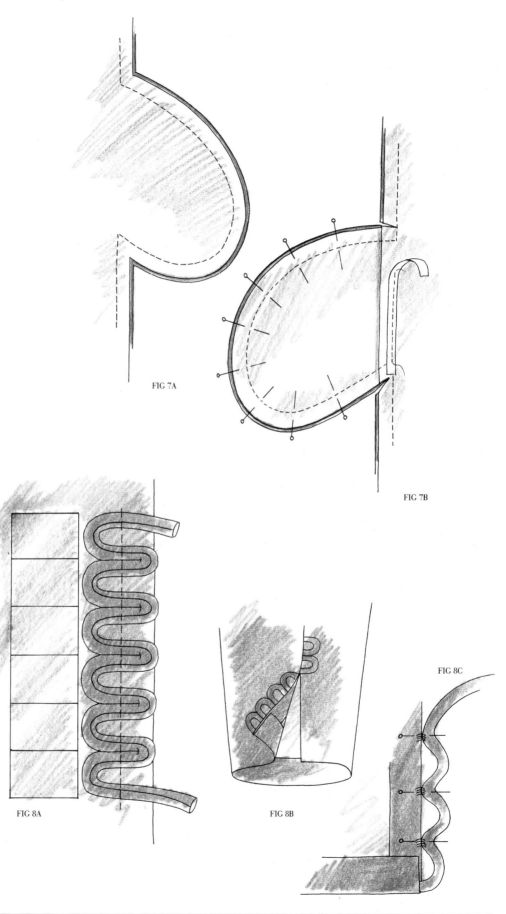

FIG 7A

FIG 7B

FIG 8A

FIG 8B

FIG 8C

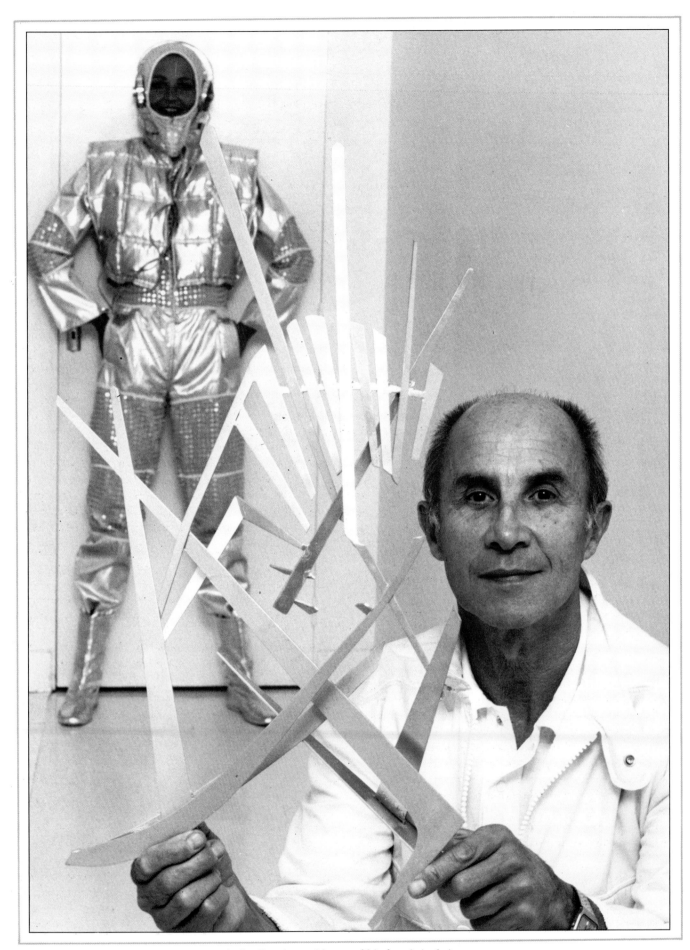

Andre Courrèges with one of his futuristic designs.

CHAPTER NINE

André Courrèges

STYLIST FOR THE FUTURE

The phenomenon of André Courrèges was perhaps short-lived, but for all that he produced a look (which he still continues in modified versions) which typified an era, and took haute couture in a startling new direction. Chronologically, he fills the time space between the demise of the grandeur of the New Look, and the more individualistic fashion which, at the top end of the market, Yves Saint Laurent personifies. Alongside Pierre Cardin, Courrèges produced that sixties 'Space Age' style which revolutionized our view of clothing. His own description of his work best explains his philosophy:

The frivolous, superficial aspects of my profession do sometimes offend me, since for me couture is not an end in itself. I truly want to bring solutions to the problems of modern women. Designing a building and making a dress have much in common. The principal concern of both is to give the impression of grace and harmony while at the same time being practical. My designs are simple and function like modern architecture.

How the designer sees himself, and how his clothes strike his audience do not always match up. Many of Courrèges' designs were considered frankly ludicrous when they first appeared, and whatever he may claim about functionalism, many of his models were fantasies – short mini-length dresses in white organdie, with flowers and bows, are hardly practical. In 1972 he even went as far as creating a collection of floor-length crinolines. But the originality of his work, and the technical perfection of many of his designs, justifies his place as one of the most significant couturiers of the present time.

André Courrèges, like his mentor, Balenciaga, was an outsider in Paris, being born in Pau, the Basque region of France, in 1923. As a young man he studied civil engineering (like many other couturiers, a career in some more formal structure-based profession was often indicated at an early age). 'I have always like to paint,' he relates in an interview given to Betty Werther, published in *Fashion, Art*

and Beauty, a book to commemorate a major exhibition including his work, at the Metropolitan Museum, New York. 'Being a staunch admirer of Le Corbusier and Saarinen, I might have become an architect had my family been able to finance my studies. They were not, and so couture has become the best way I've found to formulate my ideas.'

Set on his course, he studied textiles and fashion design first in his home town and later in Paris. In 1950, he managed to find a job with the house of Balenciaga – a significant choice, for not only did he have the Franco-Spanish element in common with his teacher, but a sympathy with the formal, structured style of tailoring which the great couturier had perfected. In the biographical sketch by Ann Ryan in *Paris Fashion* their relationship is described:

The impression he (Balenciaga) made on the young Courrèges was profound. He engaged him as a cutter and, in the ten years Courrèges remained with him, Balenciaga taught him everything, not only about couture but about life. Those ten years of hard work, amounting almost to slavery, were, I believe, the clue to his success in later years. He learnt, under the tuition of the master, to sew, to fit, and to draw.

During his years at Balenciaga, Courrèges met the woman who was to become his wife, and also his most close collaborator: Coqueline Barrière. She was an employee like himself, and with her support and active participation, he took the step to break away from Balenciaga and prepare himself for an independent career as a designer. By 1961, Courrèges was ready to launch his own collection. There has always been some debate as to whether Courrèges launched the 'mini' or whether the first to do so was Mary Quant, working concurrently with her boutique in the King's Road. Courrèges certainly was the first Parisian couturier to begin lifting the hemline. Mary Quant stylized the new desire for freedom with an irreverence, a cheap, cheeky atmosphere to her clothes which Courrèges' models never managed to convey. Instead they were demandingly daring. Courrèges' work took a few years to catch the public eye: it was not until

right *A model from the 1968 collection when Courrèges was in his 'Space Age' heyday. In spite of the trendy cutouts, the dress was as immaculately constructed and tailored as any his mentor Balenciaga had made before him.*

left *A good example of Courrèges' very structured lines, a coat from the couture collection, 1983. Symmetry, fine detail, perfect seaming have been the hallmarks of his work throughout his career. The look changes little: his ideal woman is young, muscular and neat.*

a stunning spring collection in 1964 that international fame was secured for him, almost overnight.

The clothes in predominantly pastel shades and white, were short, with cut-away areas at the midriff, over the back, and – very startling for those days – were worn on bra-less models. The fabrics he chose to work in (and which became identifiably his own) were gaberdines, flat-faced tattersalls, linens, heavy cottons, and synthetics. Silver abounded. Besides the bareness and bralessness, trouser suits with three-quarter length jackets, the legs cut so that the line fell long over the heel back, curved up over the instep, suddenly captured the fancy of the audience as the definitive uniform for the time. Yet those very first trouser suits, apparently so revolutionary and liberating, had the most immaculately wide-set collars, curving out in the Balenciaga tradition. Space helmets and the ubiquitous white kid boots completed the new picture. Courrèges commented:

> With my preoccupation for the functional, I first shortened skirts for freedom, then added the boots to keep women warm in compensation. It was only then that I discovered boots to be indispensable aesthetically.

The trouser suit revolution was exactly what women at the time needed. Nothing could be further away from the wide-skirted fashions favoured by women at the end of the war. In a way, Courrèges was sowing the seeds for the destruction of haute couture, though this much-forecast event has not actually taken place to this day. Instead a slow reversal of its power and influence is to be seen, so that present day couturiers have nothing like the international influence of Dior or Balenciaga, but still service a wealthy and discriminating clientèle. Courrèges work was pirated immediately, because it was so distinctive, and in demand. This slowly forced him, like other up-and-coming designers of the time, to consider producing his own range of ready-to-wear clothes, something that previous designers, such as Chanel and Schiaparelli had done as a side-line to their main creative output. For Courrèges, Cardin and Yves Saint Laurent, the position is exactly the opposite: their ready-to-wear is the main part of the business, their couture a 'design studio' activity.

Courrèges, likes his Italian contemporary, Valentino, always attracted the wealthiest and most glamorous women to his first small salon in the avenue Kléber. Jacqueline Kennedy paraded his little white coats, with matching boots and short white gloves, combining high fashion with decorum. Even the Duchess of Windsor bought a trouser suit. Typically, Courrèges went on record publicly saying that he did not care for the status of his clients, as long as he was paid in cash for the purchase. With this attitude it was not entirely unpredictable that when he moved to new premises in the rue François Premier in 1967, he should launch his ready-to-wear clothes, after a two year gap away from the couture collection showings. In the interim, he had gathered sufficient finance for his new expansion (partly from a French bank, partly from his wife and private patrons). Courrèges continued to consolidate his style of dressing, still producing the shift-shape dresses, the trouser suits, the immaculate evening clothes, but never quite regained the phenomenal impact his earlier collections had won. Not that he is at all deterred by the press reaction, for he has found a market, and still caters for it with assurance. Sometimes his comments on designing give the impression that he is almost remote from the world of fashion:

> Like an architect, I work on my drawing board with my models and my fabrics. I don't need to see the woman who will wear my clothes any more than an architect needs to build a house before he decides where he's going to put the windows. We can do all that on the plan. I am a technician, and drawing is my manner of philosophizing, of reflecting.

Certain examples of his work reveal the technical achievement of Courrèges perfectly. In the Victoria and Albert Museum collection, for instance, there is a light beige wool coat, dated 1967, with paler beige pockets cut in circles and mounted to the hipline of the fabric. The entire front and sleeves, likewise the back, is cut in one piece, with merely an insertion of a gusset under the arm. But the shape, which remains slim and form-fitting, is created by the use of a very narrow yoke-like section across the top of the shoulders. In another dress, an evening mini in thick gauzy fabric, appliquéd with padded flowers, the lining is constructed separately and very lightly basted in: as in the work of other couturiers, for example, Poiret, such 'space age' designs still called for a luxurious use of fabrics, the mark always of couture work. The padded organdie layer is interlined with plain white organdie, and a further fine lawn underlining is laid behind that, joined at the under-bust yoke seam. A further couture detail: on the centre-front seam, creating the flared line, the padded flowers have been carefully unpicked from the fabric, and restitched in place, overlapping the seam to conceal it.

By the 1970s, couture clothes accounted for only about ten per cent of his business, which grew massively during the previous decade, from the small house with about 60 employees to well over 500 staff, with an equal number of outworkers: more than 1000 in total. His ready-to-wear labels were *Couture Future*, for mature women (selling at about one third of couture prices), *Hyperbole* for the younger women, again selling for one fifth of couture, and knitwear designs under the name of *Maille*.

Courrèges continues to go his own way, surviving through the changes of taste that the 1980s have brought. He still has several boutiques dotted throughout Europe, but has lost the significant lead he had as a designer in the 1960s. *Vogue* thought very little of the 1982 collection 'remotely wearable'. The attraction of manufacturing his own ready-to-wear has not weaned him away from desiring acceptance and praise from his couturier colleagues. It will be interesting to see if tastes in the future catch up with Courrèges again, but even without that further accolade, his existing work ensures his international reputation.

Courrèges' so-called 'space age' fashions were tailoring triumphs. It is strange to think that designs which were so revolutionary in design concept depended as much on traditional skills in cutting cloth and finishing seams, as almost any other designs in history. Courrèges' great talent lay in his cutting: many of the dresses he created in the mid-1960s depended for their shape entirely on the cut of the various sections, with no darts – all the shaping came from the yoke shape, and the cutting of the main seamlines. (The lining of each of these dresses was cut on exactly the same lines as the body of the garment, and then hand-stitched in place.) His clothes were all finished with extreme care: the heads of zips on these modern white wool minis, for instance, would be covered with small sections of matching lining fabric, to prevent the metal rubbing against the bare skin. Another feature of many of Courrèges' designs is that they have no separate facings, as such; the sections of the garment would be folded back to neaten edges, perhaps by two or three inches, and top-stitched. Most examples of his wool clothes have surprisingly deep hems – to help create the stiff silhouette – but in spite of this modernity, the examples studied have all had hand-stitched zips.

Apart from these pointers to his skill, Courrèges also favoured a range of other techniques that he has very positively made his own, in particular, his treatment of seams for structure and decoration.

TOPSTITCHING

Topstitching is a way of decorating the edge of a fabric, either close to a facing, or round the edge of a detail, such as a patch pocket, or collar.

The first essential is that the seams on a curved area should be graded: the seam allowances inside the faced area are trimmed away in graduating layers, as shown in the diagram; the top turning would be trimmed to 3mm (⅛in), the turning below, to 6mm (¼in), just short of the usual seam allowance. This grading creates less bulk in the seams to be stitched (FIG 1).

It is important to create some guidance system with the sewing machine so that you can keep the line of the topstitching exactly parallel with the edge of the area to be worked. If the stitching falls very close to the edge of the garment, then the width of the presser foot may be sufficient to act as a guide.

Another useful device is to place a strip of masking tape on the throat plate of the sewing machine, exactly parallel with the needle and presser foot. If the facing is well basted in position, this extra guide line should ensure no wavy lines as the stitching is made (FIG 2).

An alternative method for machine-stitching a decorative line is to reverse the garment, so that the right, outer side is face down on the sewing plate. Thread the bobbin, by hand, with a thicker pearlized twist, and thread the top sewing point with a matching cotton (satinized cotton for real fabrics such as wool or heavy cotton, synthetic thread for synthetic fabrics, which have more 'give'). It is always sensible to practise on folded scraps of spare fabric (folded to the same number of layers as the actual sewing area) to ensure that the machine tension is adjusted correctly (FIG 3).

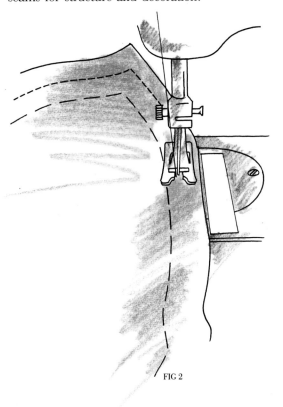

FIG 2

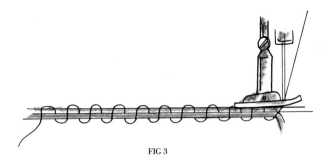

FIG 3

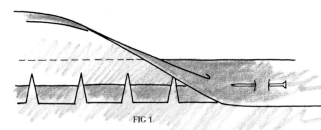

FIG 1

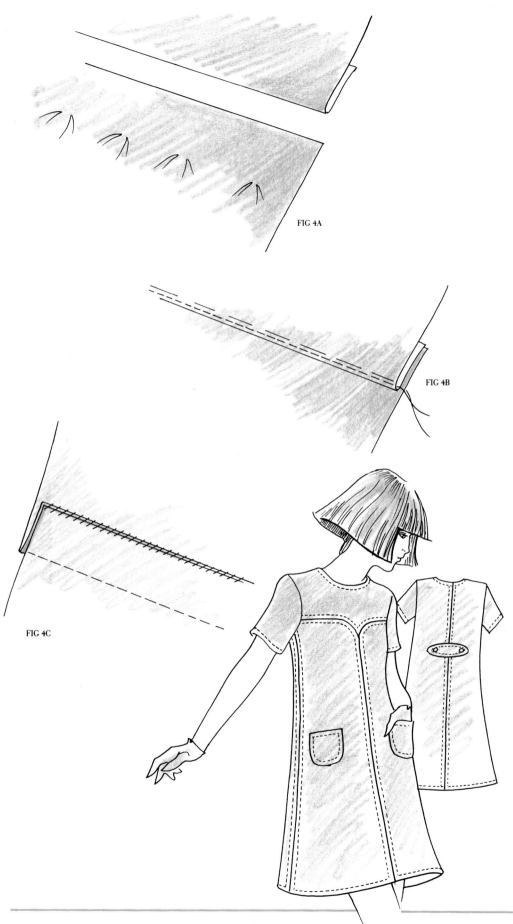

FIG 4A

FIG 4B

FIG 4C

OVERLAID SEAMS

Overlaid seaming is a method of joining fabrics that creates a pleasing raised effect to the seam. It is best handled when used on a straight grain – curving is tricky, though with more experience it can be managed. It is essential that the garment should be well-fitted, as there is no means of altering the position of the seam once it is made. Unpicking the seam will tend to pull on the fabric, and stretch it out of line, so immaculate preparatory fitting is very important.

Fold the seam allowance of the seam to be completed, back on to the wrong side. Tack along the foldline to make a sharp, crisp edge. Align this fold over the actual seaming line of the other section of fabric – for accuracy, mark down this line with tailor's chalk or tailor's tacks before separating the two layers. Place the folded edge over the marked line, pin and then baste in place. Decorative topstitching (as described above) may be used, or alternatively, an embroidery stitch, worked by machine. The two raw edges of the seam allowance can be prized out and finished by machine, or hand-neatened with an overcasting stitch (FIG 4A, 4B, 4C).

This seaming method is used by Courrèges for great effects down the outside leg of trousers, or on the top edging of yoke/shoulder seams, where a pronounced line helps to emphasize the designed shape of the garment.

CHANNEL SEAMING

This method of seam finishing became closely identified with the work of Courrèges and Cardin in the 1960s, and is comparatively easy to achieve.

In the same way as for the overlaid seam, the actual line of the join needs to be very carefully marked on both sides of the line, with tailor's chalk or tailor's tacks. Once marked, fold the edges back to the wrong side and press; this makes a firm edge without stretching or distorting the fabric (FIG 5).

Now cut a strip of fabric equal to the width of the seam allowances. Mark the centre of the strip and place this under the folded butted edges. Baste, then stitch on the two folds over the strip. Cut, then neaten the seam allowances as shown. As already noted, Courrèges tends to leave fairly wide seam turnings, much wider than those recommended by dressmaker techniques in general. You may find that for certain firm wools, this extra allowance on the margin helps the garment to maintain its shape. (The trimming away of seam allowances is a safety measure to reduce bulk on seams that are not expertly fitted.) (FIG 6A, 6B)

PIPED SEAMS

One of the most distinctive couture details is the piped seam. Though often used as an insertion into a seam, it also features as a decorative edging on a cuff or collar, even inserted into a hem panel.

Piping for fashion is much easier to manage than piping for soft furnishing, as the fabrics are much softer. It is made even simpler if you have a piping attachment on the sewing machine which will help to keep the cord exactly in place, though diligent handwork and a simple zipper foot will also provide a perfectly fine finish.

Be sure to cut the fabric used for the piping casing exactly on the bias. Make any joins that are necessary on the straight grain, otherwise the joins may tend to buckle while being handled. Form the bias strip exactly in half round the cord (which should always first be hot-washed in order to pre-shrink it). Make the fold with the right side of the fabric facing out. Once basted, machine-stitch down the casing to secure the cord in place. Attach the prepared piping to the edge to be decorated, matching up seam allowances. Notch the bias casing right up to the cord, wherever there is a corner or a curve to be completed (FIG 7A, 7B).

FIG 5

FIG 6A

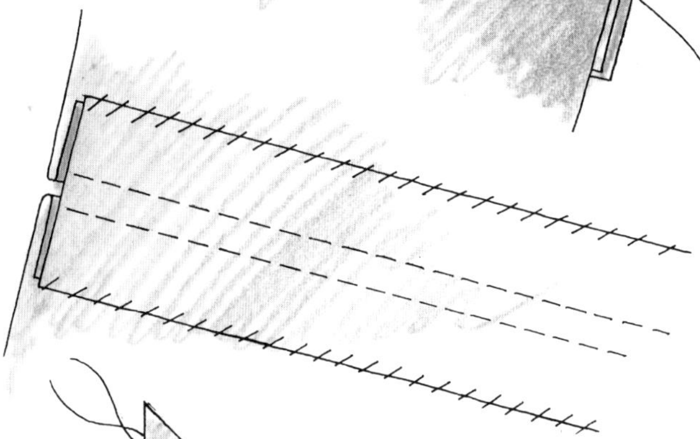

FIG 6B

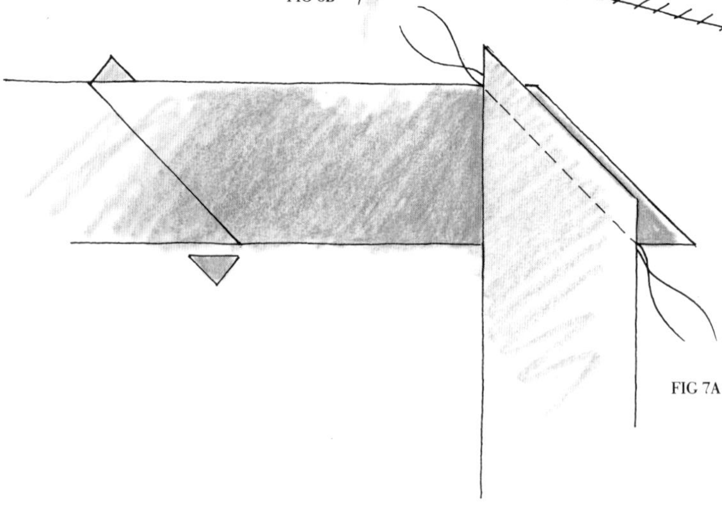

FIG 7A

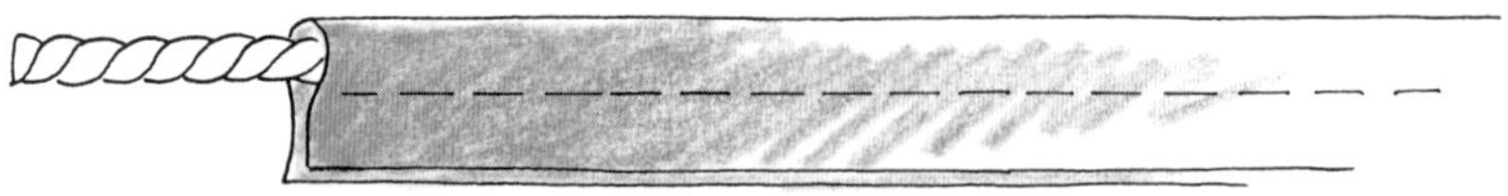

FIG 7B

Baste with small running stitches – fixing the cord firmly by hand in this way helps enormously to keep the final machine stitching perfectly in line. (If you use the right colour sewing thread rather than basting cotton, these running stitches can be left in.) Then, using the piping foot or zipper foot, machine along the basted line, keeping as close to the piping as possible. Most piped joining seams are finished by oversewing the four raw edges (FIG 8A, 8B).

Couturiers often use the piped seams where they are combining fabrics of different weight, to give structural strength to the seam – the lighter fabric does not pull away or pucker, against the heavier fabric. For example, Poiret inserted a piped seam between areas of stiff brocade and soft satin, in the sleeve sections of a kimono coat (FIG 9).

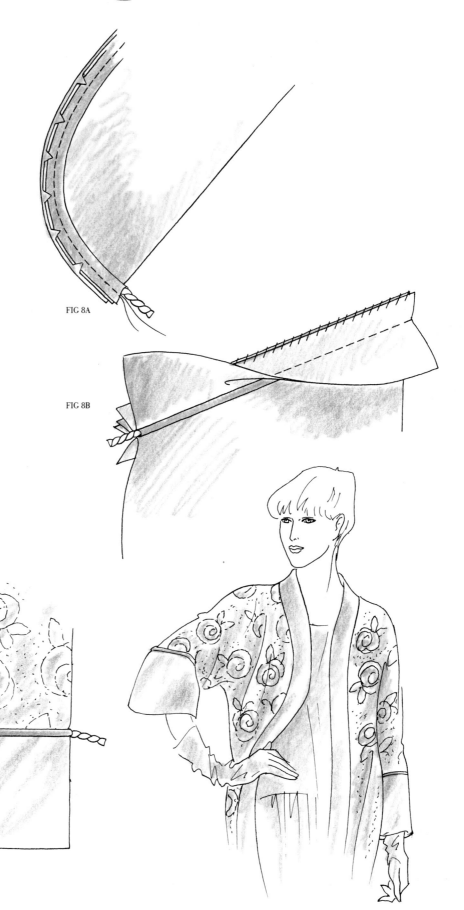

FIG 8A

FIG 8B

FIG 9

Pierre Cardin at work on one of his recent collections, 1983.

CHAPTER TEN

Pierre Cardin

INVENTOR WITH FLAIR

As a spokeswoman for *Vogue* magazine once said, Pierre Cardin's attitude to his designing work could be summed up succinctly in the words, 'When in doubt, license it'. In comparison with the other contemporary designers covered in this survey, Cardin has survived the vicissitudes of the haute couture world better than most. But, then as the examples of his work on these pages show, he is endlessly inventive – and perhaps equally important, more able than some of his colleagues to keep one step ahead of changing tastes, without losing his own distinctive touch. His creative talent is matched by an equal energy for business – which is why he has remained in the forefront of French fashion for two decades. His reputation in his own country is enormous, much greater than in the UK or USA, perhaps because his clothes are too 'chic', too glamorously smart for Anglo-Saxon tastes.

Pierre Cardin was born in Italy, in 1923, to French parents. He grew up in Venice, but returned to Paris, where after a brief flirtation with commerce, working as a book-keeper, he found an opening at the long-established house of Paquin, where his basic training as a couturier took place. He worked subsequently at Schiaparelli, and then at the house of Dior – where it was once possible that he might have inherited the mantle, which Yves Saint Laurent took instead. It is interesting that the two most enduring modern designers should have run neck and neck, out of the same stable.

Cardin opened his own salon in 1953. His work owes much to his careful tailoring background: finely sculptured shapes, with immaculate edging details, such as stitched collars, scalloped facings to suits, curved blouson-effect overblouses, and shift-shaped dresses with sculptured forms cut out of their sides. In spite of producing some revolutionary dressing concepts (such as the tubular moulded knit dresses, launched in 1966) Cardin shows all the hallmarks of a classic couturier in the detailed craftsmanship so clear in his work. As Serena Sinclair (fashion editor of London's *Daily Telegraph*) wrote in *Paris Fashion*:

> These signatures of the couturiers are fascinating to recognize, for like the motifs on the ruins or the artefacts of an ancient civilisation, they are the instant mark of their taste. Cardin will be known to future archaeologists by his giant collars and the geometric detail of his dresses.

In 1967, for example, Cardin created a tube of a dress in black crêpe, suspending it from the neck of the model by attaching it to a finely cast metal neckpiece. The design was simultaneously primitive in origin, like an African queen's robe, and yet strangely modern. The same is true for the stitchery magic which he can employ on appliquéd pockets, topstitched collars and revers: their origins may be ancient (Elizabethan ruffs or Renaissance padded clothes) but the final effect is positively futuristic. There have been times, however, when his vision has been frankly out of keeping with the taste of the moment. As early as 1957 he produced a separate menswear line, and has promoted the use of knitted fabrics, in body stockings, all-in-one stretch suits, and tabard-like sleeveless tops over stretchy leggings for men as well as women. All that survived from this innovation was the brief vogue for polo-necks under suit jackets. In 1959 he shocked Paris by launching his own women's ready-to-wear line. Now all the couturiers do it.

As is often the case with a designer as prolific as Cardin (many fashion journalists complain about the length and weariness of his shows) for every idea that does not take on, half a dozen others will be seen as ready-to-wear clothes, five, ten years later. Looking at Cardin designs of the sixties and seventies, there are many shapes and details that look as fresh to the eye today as when they were first shown to the public. A Cardin suit with tab pockets, a mean collar with narrow top-stitched revers, and a front-slit skirt, designed in 1964, would with little difficulty find itself in a current

right *Cardin in his 'Space Age' phase, Autumn 1966. The semi-circular cut-outs were a signature of the time. But tailoring still conforms to old principles.*

below *A simple coat shape, cut on the bias, with a padded rolled hem that adds to the impression of movement. Apparently simple, the coat is very carefully constructed. Cardin insists that his real work is as a couturier or simple 'dressmaker'.*

wardrobe as a fashionable version of sharp, punk styling. (In fact a similar suit turned up in his 1978 collection, to which Cardin replies, 'Sure I've made a few "quotations" of myself, but, that's only so I don't make the other couturiers look out of date.') The stand-up, stand-away turtleneck collars and the hats with curved-back brims fit equally as easily into the current taste for 'good feel' fabrics, and pioneer American accessories. As for the evening clothes, the sculptured, dateless shapes have as much energy now as ever. He has been described as 'a design factory for all Paris', and the wealth of ideas thronging his output justifies the remark.

It is not merely in his cutting and styling that Cardin has proved innovatory, but in his accessorizing too. The hats were always eye catching: head-hugging skull caps, boaters, or helmet shapes. His use of new fabrics, particularly vinyl, became a signature – appliquéd in circles or diamonds onto the midriff of dresses. Textured stockings, to match the colour and feel of a dress fabric, were primarily his idea, though now this fashion seems ubiquitous.

In the late 60s, Cardin's export business, selling exclusives for ready-to-wear lines, was second only to Dior. Licences in every imaginable field have continued to build up throughout the 70s and 80s: first menswear, Cardin suits (on which he receives a royalty) besides bedlinen, watches, cars, perfumes, stockings, even the interior of a Johnson and Johnson aeroplane. He has always been preoccupied with 'space' – linked with Courrèges as one of the 'Space Age' designers, originally, he christened his own fashion showing theatre – a refurbished old nightclub theatre – L'Espace! In its all-white interior, buyers and journalists sit crowded and stunned as a non-stop stream of inventive ideas run down the catwalk. Even with the passage of time, it appears that Cardin's energy does not diminish. In January 1982, he showed a remarkably beautiful and varied collection, totalling 320 models, in just under *two* hours. That same month, he bought an additional two million dollars' worth of shares in the famous French restaurant, Maxims. Maxim's is now open in Paris, totally re-designed and refurbished by Cardin, and there are plans to open a similar establishment, with the same name, in London late in 1983. Cardin also owns twelve shops in Paris.

Also in 1982, Cardin received the extraordinary distinction of being the only couturier to be invited to China to show his collection, and to give the Chinese some idea of the highest western manifestation of the art of dressmaking. His collection was especially scaled down to be shown on a handful of smaller Japanese models, and the showing was staged in one of the pavilions of the ancient Palace of Abstinence, in the Temple of the Sky in Peking. 'Pi Er Ca Dan', as he was called (Pierre le Rouge) completely stunned his audience with the glamour and other-worldliness of his designs. The official reaction however was a genuine one: while the Chinese need not adopt the values and the style of the West, they could certainly learn the techniques required for their own industry from such a great exponent of couture. The result was that Cardin has opened a boutique, in the main thoroughfare of the city of Peking, and has finalized an agreement to set up a factory, to produce Cardin-licensed designs (for domestic consumption but also for export trade). And in exchange, what will he receive? Royalties, in the form of high quality silks and cashmeres, 'thus eliminating the need for banking' as the *New York Times* commented at the time. Cardin himself takes a realistic attitude to relationship with the various operations in which he moves: a designer must produce ideas, and a steady flow of them, before the question of markets and how to deal with them, even appears. He declares:

> I am as much Cardin as Chanel is Chanel. Firstly, one has to have the idea – it's the inspiration that counts. What I do is really, dressmaking, *couture*. If you haven't got patronage, then you will achieve nothing. It has nothing to do with trimmings, yards of lace, etc. Everything comes down to the cut.

Only a man with as much gift for invention as Cardin can survey contemporary fashion, and condemn the excesses that so often appear:

> There's a terrible lack of order in haute couture at the moment. It seems as if fashion is heading towards a collapse without any sense of direction. It needs a directing idea, and then that must suit all the women of today, the younger ones as much as the older ones.

At least Cardin is still offering new possibilities, not merely re-defining contemporary looks. One of his most original and flattering outlines came in the 1979–80 collection, where he showed wide, straight shoulders, lightly padded, but also squared through the cut of the sleeve head and shoulder line, falling down into a soft, loosely fitting bodice and turning into an asymmetrically cut skirt, high-slashed on one side, and dropping low on the other. Beneath the skirt, which creates a very attractive hip and leg line, Cardin placed narrow-legged trousers, Indian in style. The total outfit is practical, but also very flattering.

In 1982, having worked on the square shoulder line for several collections, Cardin turned to another shape completely. He showed several beautiful suits with domed and rounded sleeve heads, and one complex design where the edge of the sleeveless jacket seemed to spiral round the armhole, ending up caught into the waistband. Full sleeves for the blouse complemented the shape. Several other dresses in this collection were narrow in line. On tailoring, Cardin says: 'When I use an expensive fabric, I cut it into a very narrow dress. I am a creator, that's true, but I'm also the boss and the financial director'.

Cardin is unusual in his combination of creativity and business acumen: he seems to have the steeliness necessary for running his own empire without any sacrifice of his artistic sensitivity. His craftsmanship, the continuous search for new shapes, finishes, and outlines, is outstanding. It is difficult to understand quite why his position, virtually an unofficial ambassador for France, is so elevated in his own country, and not matched outside. The view given in *Le Quotidien* 27 January 1981 shows the enthusiasm the French feel for him:

> Once more, Pierre Cardin shows us what he can do with the classic and couture, research and couture, youth and couture. This is not always the case with individuals. He is a '*diable d'homme*' [literally, a devil of a man] whom we should thank every day, for his existence.

Perhaps our prejudice against art meddling with commerce tells against Pierre Cardin – he offends against these rules, being able to shine at both simultaneously. (John Fairchild, of *Women's Wear Daily*, has referred to Cardin recently as 'that restauranteur' to explain why he no longer goes to see his collections.) As recent examples of Cardin's work show, this view is entirely unmerited, the world of fashion still having everything to gain from an appreciation of Cardin's great style.

Pierre Cardin is so prolific a designer, and such a master technician, that to choose only one aspect of his work is to do him a disservice. Besides, some of his output is too complicated for copying: his recent work with sleeves, for example, is the result of years of experimentation, and emulating it would be far beyond the ability of any but the most skilful dressmaker, the secret lying in the cut. The techniques he uses for his extremely elegant hem finishes, on the other hand, create fewer problems.

A perfectly made hand-worked hem sets a garment apart from the ready-to-wear product. Even the most expensive clothes nowadays have machine-stitched hems – something that an observant eye cannot fail to find offensive. Altering a hem to create a decorative feature can not only add drama to a dress or skirt, but will often bring out the character of a fabric in a way that other finishing techniques cannot – particularly if you use a zigzag hem edge for a zigzag fabric design, or smooth scallops either to complement a wavy pattern or to set off a beautiful plain fabric. (For a couture hem see page 105; for a handrolled hem see page 122; for a hem suitable for nets and laces, see page 123.) The scalloped hem shown below was used on several Cardin models.

A SCALLOPED HEM

The first step in the making of a scalloped hem is to prepare the edge of the fabric by machining round the curve with a fine row of stitches, close to the edge. This is also the first essential for making an *eased* hem: the threads are slightly gathered up to allow the fullness of the hem turning to be evenly distributed around the hem area. The gathers can then be gently eased away by using a damp cloth and light pressure from an iron. For a plain edge, finish with the couture stitch shown on page 79 (FIG 1).

To make a scalloped edge, the following stages should be followed. Trim the hem to about 2.5cm (1in) from the stitched line, cutting evenly all round the skirt.

Make a bias-cut strip 2.5cm (1in) longer than the hem circumference, making any necessary joins on the straight grain of the fabric. Then, placing right sides together, pin this strip to the hem area, and baste close to the bottom edge and the top edge – about 1cm (½in) from the top and bottom of the facing piece. Try to position the joins in the facing on top of the joins in the skirt seams if possible (take this into account when preparing the bias strip in the first place: measure the distance between seams and try to cut the bias strips to fit.) (FIG 2)

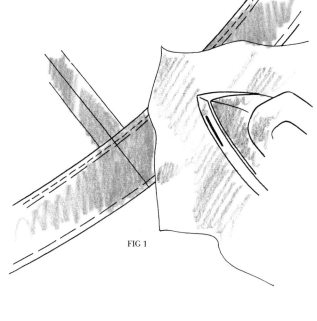

FIG 1

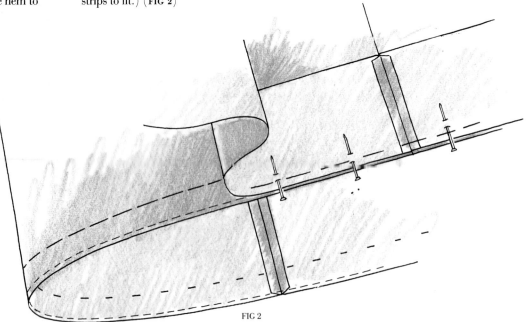

FIG 2

FIG 3

FIG 4

FIG 5

Measure the circumference of the skirt once again, and work out a scallop width that will divide precisely into this figure. Using a compass, or failing that any other round template shape you can cut from card to fit this diameter, mark round the facing, on the wrong side, with the template, using French chalk. Each scallop can correspond exactly to the half-circle of the template, or you can vary the curve, according to taste, making a shallower shape if you prefer. As with the seaming in the skirt, it is a good idea, if possible, to make the corner between the scallops fall exactly on the skirt seams. Make small running stitches round the shapes, to act as a sewing guide.

Machine, using a small stitch, making sure that you pivot the needle to form a uniformly shaped point in the gap between each scallop as you work. Once the stitching is completed, trim away the excess fabric round the scallops and snip notches very carefully into the remaining allowance, to give plenty of ease when the scallops are turned out (FIG 3).

The same basic method is used for making a hem with points, or any other regular or irregular shape that comes to mind. The key detail that gives these hem finishes that inherent style is to measure carefully, and adjust the size of the individual shape to fit the hem circumference perfectly (FIG 4).

Once the scallops or other shapes have been stitched and cut out, turn the facing through to the underside of the hem. Use the points of a closed pair of scissors to push out the shapes evenly and fully. (FIG 5)

Some Cardin designs have topstitching applied to the curve of the scallops – on one example the curving line of stitching was shallower than the scallop itself, adding greater interest to the shapes. This helps to keep the scallops well-shaped, too (FIG 6).

All that then remains is to finish the top edge of the hem facing. Apply a very light bias-cut binding to the raw edge, and stitch the hem using the couture technique, described on page 105. If the fabric is substantial and firm, then you can run a line of fine stitching close to the edge of the facing, then trim down to it with pinking shears, and slip-stitch the facing into place without binding (FIG 7A, 7B).

For an even more precise finish to the scallops, you can edge-stitch the shapes by making tiny stitches into the facing and the seam allowances inside the hem. Make sure, however, that the stitches do not come through to the right side of the fabric (FIG 8).

On very lightweight fabrics, a facing can be omitted altogether: follow the instructions for cutting out the shapes on the edge of the garment, and decorate them with a very narrow and soft bias trim, making a neat fold between each curve. Such a hem would have to be hand-sewn for a perfect finish.

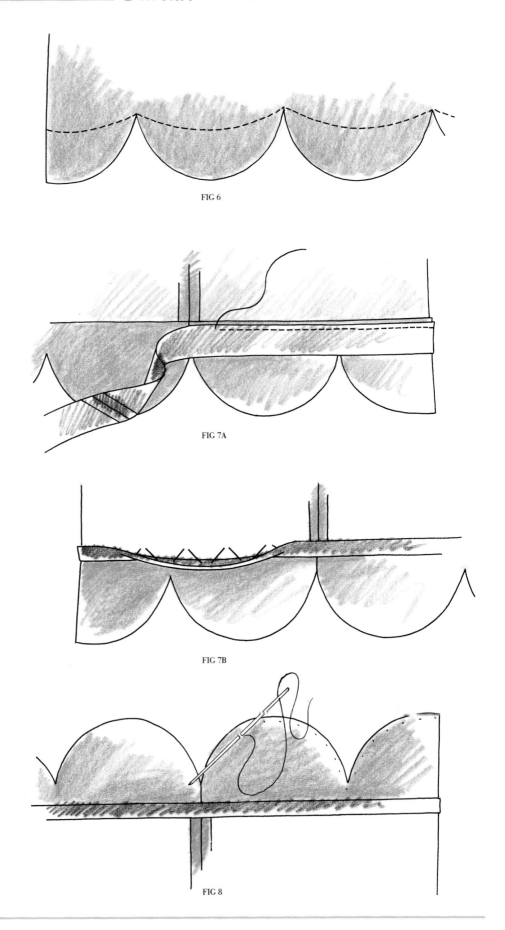

FIG 6

FIG 7A

FIG 7B

FIG 8

A ROLLED OR PADDED HEM

Couture garments are often distinguishable from those that have been mass-produced by having a padded hem, rather than a sharply-creased edge. To achieve this effect, the hem is interfaced, the top edge of the bias-cut strip being secured with a wide herringbone stitch, or catch-stitch. The strip should be just the width of the hem turning, plus an extra 1cm (½in) below the notional foldline. Secure the lower edge with basting. To achieve the required padded effect, extra fleecing or polyester wadding can then be carefully basted into place over the interfacing, just on and above the hem line, as shown (FIG 9A, 9B).

The actual hem edge should be finished as previously described, with a bias-trimmed, couture hem.

A FRILLY HEM

Cardin is one of the few modern designers who explores synthetics to create interesting new designs. As a complete contrast then to the foregoing hem ideas, which are structured and suitable for woven fabrics, here is one that works very well for stretch fabrics. It has been widely adopted in recent years by couturiers, especially Cardin and Yves Saint Laurent, and high-class ready-to-wear designers, such as Jean Muir and Zandra Rhodes, as a technique eminently suitable to these relatively new materials.

To achieve a good finish with this hem, it is wise to practise the stitching first on a scrap of fabric, so that you arrive at a zigzag setting that does not cause the fabric to curl on itself.

There can be no mistakes with this hem: make doubly sure of the length you prefer, before cutting the fabric, as you must cut to exactly the length required, with a tiny allowance of 2mm (⅛in) for trimming away after stitching. Begin by marking along the stitching line very accurately with tailor's chalk. Then, commence the stitching on the machine, slightly stretching the fabric as you work. It takes some practice and a little dexterity to ensure that you stretch the fabric more or less evenly on each section as it is worked. The end result will be improved if you can manage this (FIG 10).

If the fabric you are using frays very badly, you can, as an alternative method, flip over the margin of 2mm (⅛in) with your thumb nail, on to the wrong side, and machine stitch through the fold. Any extra fabric emerging from the stitching can be trimmed away very carefully with small sharp scissors, to avoid a raggedy look (FIG 11).

Once the stitching has been completed, the finished hem produces a frilled edge, which is particularly attractive on lightweight jerseys.

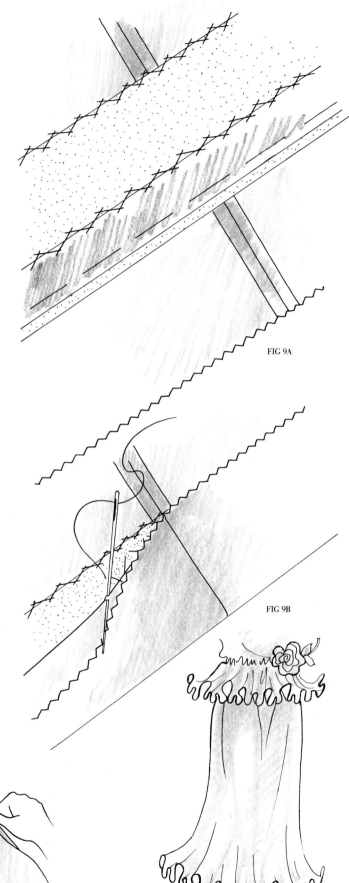

FIG 9A

FIG 9B

FIG 10

FIG 11

An Yves Saint Laurent design, sharply detailed, 1981.

Hard chic generally excludes anything sexy, perhaps that is why designers now don't get it right: most people prefer to look alluring. Very few designers can pull off an elegant sexy look, but when they can it's sensational. Chanel could. Saint Laurent can.

Janey Ironside (head of London's Royal College of Art's fashion department) gave this view of Saint Laurent's peculiar talent to *Vogue* magazine in May 1973. Exactly a decade later, Yves Saint Laurent is still being acclaimed as one of the leading and most exciting designers working in Paris. Serena Sinclair's report on the Paris haute couture collections in Spring 1983 for the London *Daily Telegraph* opened with exactly the same notion:

Chic's the word: it's all cut and drape. The new sleek Paris looks terrific. Couture is alive and healthy, showing the way ahead with just a nod or two (maybe too many) towards the forties and fifties.

Saint Laurent contributed two new lines to the season's look: a scoop-necked tunic blouse in a splashy print, over a slim white skirt, and a coat-dress in navy gaberdine, 'sparked with an enormous crystal choker'. The details are important because they bring together the elements that have always made Saint Laurent's work successful. He likes always to glance over his shoulder – no one has revived 'looks' with more originality than Saint Laurent. He uses tailored shapes too – pleated skirts, pencil-slim silhouettes to dresses – but always adds a softening, glamorous detail like the bead choker, or a silk scarf, to relieve the hard edge of the chic.

The parallel drawn by Janey Ironside between Yves Saint Laurent and Chanel is relevant here: Chanel too managed to soften the smartness of her clothes with feminine detail. Yves Saint Laurent also shares with her the doubtful distinction of not being considered truly innovative, in the sense that the word could be applied to Poiret, or Courrèges, for example. His clothes have never wandered far from classic shapes, but

altered to suit the taste of the moment. Often his ideas are so apt that they remain a part of the slower-moving ready-to-wear scene for many years after: like the velvet blazer over the patterned dress (1970); the mannish trouser suits he made in 1973; the so-called '*naive chemises*' or shift dresses, dating from 1975, and the now popular 'waspie' corsets worn with shorts or big gathered skirts, first shown in the 'Spanish' collection of 1976.

Saint Laurent, like his contemporary, Valentino, was one of those young men for whom fashion had always had a fascination. His family lived in Algeria, where he was born in 1936. Strongly professional in tradition – his father was in insurance and his grandfather had been a lawyer – they acknowledged his talent without opposition. He arrived in Paris for the first time to enter his chosen field at the age of 17. Such was the promise visible in his portfolio of drawings that when he showed them to Michel de Brunhoff, editor of French *Vogue*, the man lost no time in securing him an interview with his friend, Christian Dior. As Dior himself had always worked from sketches in this way, he could see Saint Laurent's potential, and took him on at once. Inside the house Saint Laurent was able to learn the tailoring skills of a couturier from one of the last great exponents of the art.

His eye for modernity was probably the reason why he was chosen by Christian Dior as his successor and he worked very closely with the great couturier during the last few years before his death in 1958. Yves Saint Laurent then found himself at the head of the largest, most famous and successful couture establishment in the world. His very first independent collection fully lived up to the public expectations his position as Dior's 'Dauphin' had aroused: the Trapeze line was hailed a complete triumph. But a year later, he succumbed to the current street crazes in fashion and showed bubble skirts and motor cycle jackets, in snakeskin. Just as the journalists had praised him, they took equal delight in condemnation. With unfortunate timing (some rumours even suggesting that rival factions within the house

right
The golden boy of the youth cult, Yves Saint Laurent in the safari-style suit which he popularized in the 1960s. Then it seemed that the centre of power and creativity had shifted down ten years at least. Saint Laurent was only 22 when he inherited Dior's mantle, but the arrangement did not last. Only when he launched independently did success stay with him.

of Dior actually brought official attention to bear on him) Saint Laurent was drafted into the army for long-postponed military service. The conjunction of events – the bitter pressures and criticisms that weighed on him at Dior, the press reactions, the stiff system of the French army caused a severe nervous collapse. However, his subsequent mentor and business manager, Pierre Bergé, commented drily on one occasion that Saint Laurent was 'born with a nervous breakdown'.

Bergé's entry on the scene was vital. He had worked as manager and publicist previously for the painter, Bernard Duffet, and met Saint Laurent when the latter was 21. He recognized the potential in his young friend, and has stuck with him ever since. Today, Saint Laurent employs 300 workers in Paris alone, has over 50 manufacturing licence arrangements, and about 160 Saint Laurent Rive Gauche boutiques all over the world. All this is really Bergé's doing: Saint Laurent still finds the life of a couturier pressured and tough. Bergé enables him to escape from the difficulties and keep to his own best work.

Saint Laurent's first step on coming out of the army was to sue the house of Dior for replacing him with Marc Bohan during his absence. He won the case, and was awarded substantial damages, which he used to start up his own house. Bergé approached J. Mack Robinson, a wealthy businessman from Atlanta, Georgia. He advanced (secretly) one million dollars to launch Saint Laurent, being the principal figure in a conglomerate of investors from both sides of the Atlantic, but agreeing to keep his contribution to investment without any to artistic involvement.

Saint Laurent opened in 1962, at 30 bis rue Spontini, with Helena Rubinstein, supposedly one of his original backers, buying 16 outfits from his first collection alone. His interest in 'street' fashions gave Paris their first glimpse of an irreverent style of couture. Many of his early designs verged on fancy dress: in 1963 he showed black ciré coats with thigh-length alligator boots; in 1965 a 'Mondrian' collection of shift-like dresses, chopped into blocks of colour. In 1966 the look was built on dresses for a Moroccan gypsy, in 1969, 'highwayman' romantic coats.

In all his collections, Saint Laurent reveals that nervous sensitive aspect of his nature: no other couturier responds to changing moods on the outside world more overtly. Sometimes his work becomes sombre, even dull, if he feels that the

left *A Mondrian-inspired dress, 1965, that appealed to the popular taste for bold designs. Copies were made all over Europe. It was one of a number of 'looks' verging on fancy dress that Saint Laurent offered with style. The gipsy look, 1969, was perhaps the most pervasive in influence.*

right *The Moroccan influence is a source frequently used for shapes, colours, fabrics. But here, in 1976, Saint Laurent uses incredibly expensive and exclusive fabric so that his design cannot be exactly manufactured elsewhere. The balance between couture and ready-to-wear now is delicate but important. Couture is for the few very rich, but it also a 'design studio' for new ideas in clothes.*

climate outside is inappropriate for frills and glamour. At times this tendency has caused him to think of abandoning custom work altogether; and when couture looked as if it were finally entering its death throes in 1971, Saint Laurent announced that he would show model clothing no longer, but concentrate all his efforts into his ready-to-wear first launched in 1966 and called Saint Laurent Rive Gauche. But he never fully abandoned his work as a couturier, even though, in 1975, he considered that haute couture had only another five years to live. He explained his attitude:

> In these times it cannot last. But I feel it is my duty to perpetuate its unique qualities of craftsmanship for as long as possible. I agree that haute couture is reserved for a very few people who can afford the price and who live a certain sort of life. But what the people who attack it don't seem to understand is that I have 200 workers here. You must give these workers work . . . you must work for rich people.

It may be true that the clientele for couture is dwindling: in 1965, 15,000 women could buy it, while by the end of the seventies the figure had dropped to around a mere 400. But the main reason why designers like Saint Laurent continue to produce a couture range, however small, is that it is essential to have a platform for their more original ideas, not merely to cater for the larger ready-to-wear market. The fight against the encroachments of the garment industry takes many forms. In recent years, perhaps succumbing to the influence of Arab money, couture has become astonishingly expensive. In 1976, for example, Saint Laurent created, appropriately, a 'Berber' look – but in fabrics so exclusive and expensive that they could not be copied except in line.

Saint Laurent's statements about fashion are best balanced by looking at his actual output in recent years. Suffice it to say that both the couture and the Rive Gauche operations are thriving. In recent years, the couture collections have produced some pretty, luxurious ideas, instantly translated into mass market fashions, in spite of Rive Gauche. In 1977 he produced frilled, square-yoked dresses, reminiscent of Edwardian pinafored girls in prints. In 1978, he went back to the Hollywood 'tuxedo' look, much favoured in general at the time, but as usual brought out a new angle by making the lounging shape in soft leather, as opposed to black wool cloth or satin, like everyone else. That year also saw one of his more hilarious collections, living up to his reputation for fancy dress in extremes. It was christened the 'Porgy and Bess' collection, earning the title from the short, 'bellhop' jacket, angled hats, junk jewellery and hot, tropical colours. In 1978 he produced 'slip' dress, very much like the current trend for petticoat shapes, but perfectly set off with light, tailored jackets. There are times, however, when Saint Laurent comes so close to current tendencies that he is even accused of plagiarism. In 1980 he found himself attacked by the chief designer at Esterel over the originality of the 'matador suits' launched that year. Bergé, on behalf of Saint Laurent, rode out the storm with a mixture of unconcern and arrogant insults. Not entirely

above A more classic outfit – pleats and frills have always been superbly well executed by Saint Laurent, both in couture and Rive Gauche clothing.

Chanel often indicated that she thought Saint Laurent nearest to her values in designing chic and simple clothes, and he has her quality of workmanship.

surprisingly, the knickerbocker length trousers have become widespread street fashion ever since.

Even Saint Laurent's shifting position on couture and ready-to-wear is a demonstration of his sensitivity to the current mood. Perhaps his recent successes point the way to a future where excellent quality and extremely high standards of workmanship will again rule the day. It is no coincidence that one of the leading figures of the French ready-to-wear ascendancy during the seventies, Karl Lagerfeld, has just recently been appointed as chief designer to the house of Chanel. Coco herself said of Saint Laurent – an oft-repeated but still amusing remark: 'The poor boy might turn out all right if he simply copied me and cut his hair.' The hair was cut short long ago; the Chanel tradition certainly lives on, in Saint Laurent's glamorous and wearable designs.

Following in the tradition of classic couturiers like Chanel, Yves Saint Laurent has always created dresses and suits of a timeless elegance. In contrast to designers like Cardin, he has not been an innovator of form, but rather worked within the familiar outlines, varying styles by colour, combinations of fabrics, and adding a new zest to traditional wear. It was Saint Laurent, for instance, who first paired a blazer with a pleated day dress – a new 'suit' that broke with convention while using conventional shapes. Saint Laurent is also a master of finery: to exemplify his techniques, here are some notes on how to make perfect pleats, and how to make frills, for more fanciful creations of your own.

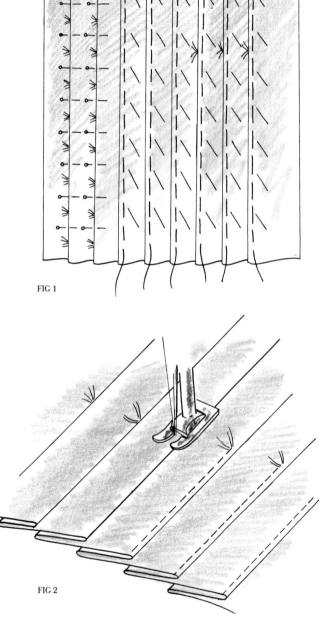

FIG 1

FIG 2

PLEATS

Two points to bear in mind when making a garment with pleats: first, the choice of fabric is totally crucial. There is no point attempting to make crisp pleats with a fabric that is not firm, able to be pressed into a clean line, it must have sufficient body to hang well. One of the reasons that couture clothes look so fine is that they are made from fabulous fabrics: if they are mis-cut or mistreated in any way, the fabric has enough 'bounce' literally to stand up and protest – particularly with gathered or pleated areas – indicating that it is not lying properly, along the true grain. This leads to the second point – pleats only lie well if the garment itself has been fitted properly, something which home dressmakers often fail to take into account.

The dress or skirt should always be fitted with the pleated area basted firmly shut, so that it only needs to be opened to give a swing to the garment, not actually to allow room for manoeuvre. For example, a skirt with an inverted front pleat should fit as if it were a straight skirt, with no pulling across the hips. This means that when the pleat is released, it will be able to fall naturally into a vertical semi-shut position.

There are various types of pleats, knife, box or inverted pleats, all of which are formed by following the same basic technique.

FORMING THE PLEATS FOR A SKIRT

It is a good idea to transfer as many basting lines as are required on to the skirt material, so that the pleats can be formed accurately. Mark the seam line round the waist, so that when the pleats are

formed, this will always remain straight and uninterrupted. Make sure the skirt section is pinned accurately to the straight grain of the fabric, and mark the line of the fold for each pleat with tailor's chalk, a dressmaker's wheel, or better still with loose basting stitches.

Also mark the line where any topstitching on the right side of the pleat will come. Folding the pleats should be done on a big flat surface – the floor or table top. Pin at frequent intervals, making sure that the fold line remains constantly in line with the basting threads. Once accurately folded, baste down the length of each pleat. As mentioned before, always work your basting lines in one direction, top to bottom. As an extra precaution to prevent the pleats from shifting or opening when you press the fabric, make diagonal basting stitches through the body of each pleat using silk thread which does not mark (FIG 1).

Pleats can be finished in a number of ways. For example, once the waistband has been added, the basting stitches can be removed, to leave unpressed pleats that swing open from the waist. A second method is to use the guidelines marked on the skirt to topstitch the pleats down to hip level, always topstitch from the hipline up to the waist for a perfect finish. Pleats can also be edge-stitched to give a firm line, but this is a style more suited to sportswear than to formal styles. A useful alternative is to edge-stitch the pleats on the underside only, helping to give them shape without any stitching being visible from the top (FIG 2).

A useful technique when making inverted pleats is to reduce the bulk in the garment,

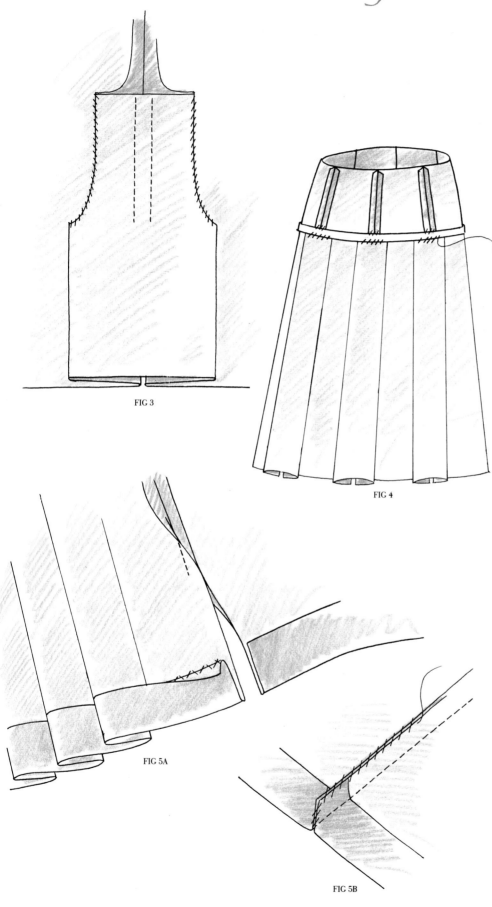

FIG 3

FIG 4

FIG 5A

FIG 5B

in the area over the stomach or hips for example, by cutting away the fold at the back of the pleat, for as far as the topstitching on the outside extends. Make a curving cut through the surplus pleats, as shown, and hand-oversew these edges, to prevent fraying (FIG 3).

A second tailoring tip for pleats that fall from a seam at the hip, is to reinforce them with a strip of 2.5cm (1in) wide firm, straight binding over the hip seam. Very carefully hem-stitch the back of each pleat to the binding, and attach the other edge of the binding to the seam allowance and any vertical seam allowances there may be. This 'belted' effect acts as a secondary band, replacing the waistband. A neat effect can also be obtained by making a skirt lining piece to the same dimensions as the hip section, and stitching the back of the pleats to the folded-under lower edge. The top edge will be mounted into the waistband (joined and darted in exactly the same way as the skirt section itself) (FIG 4).

HEMMING A PLEATED SKIRT

If possible, any joins in the side seams of the skirt should be arranged so that the seam falls at the back of a pleat join. When the skirt is assembled, the hem is finished *before* this vertical seam is completed (you can make up the skirt, leaving the bottom open at the side seams, so that you can fit and check the length of the skirt before completing this step). When the hem is finished, stitch through the side seam, and then cut or fold the two hem allowance areas at a slant, as illustrated. Hand-finish this with a small overcasting stitch (FIG 5A, 5B).

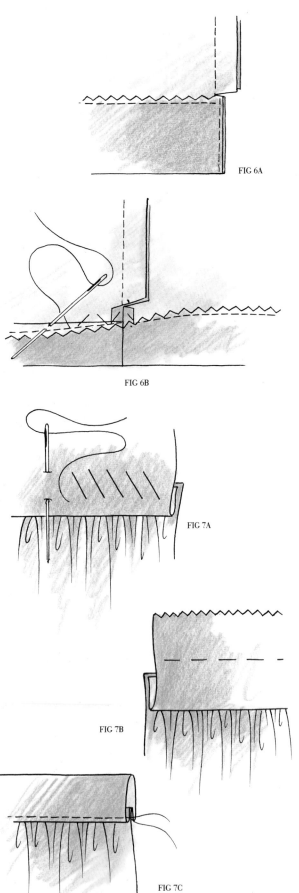

FIG 6A

FIG 6B

FIG 7A

FIG 7B

FIG 7C

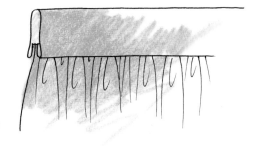

FIG 7D

Another method for finishing the hem on a pleated skirt where there is a seam at the fold, is to cut the seam allowance just above the finished hemline. Press back the seam allowance inside the folded hem area, and trim them to half the usual width to reduce bulk. Make small stitches through the edge of the side seam, on the wrong side, as shown, to help keep the pleat flat. Oversew the cut edges of the seam allowance, to prevent fraying (FIG 6A).

The hemming method used for a pleated skirt should involve the least bulk possible: if the fabric is firm, it can be pinked or oversewn on the raw edge, to avoid a double turn. Run a line of fine machine stitches just below the neatened edge. Baste the hem turning to the required depth, then slip-stitch the hem turning to the fabric the couturier way. The stitches are invisible from the front and from the hem side, and do not rub or catch on things, as other regular hemstitches are inclined to (FIG 6B).

GATHERS

The preparation of gathers for a skirt or frill is a comparatively simple operation, but there are one or two points to remember,

that will enhance your working with this technique. Firstly it is essential when sewing the running stitches for the gathering up lines, to make at least two, preferably three lines, so that the gathers will be small, puffy and more evenly dispersed along the edge. A very good method for attaching gathers into a waistband is to run one line of basting stitches, through the gathers and the band, in the usual way, but then to fold back the seam allowance, and place the band on top of the gathered frill area. Baste along the edge, and also through the band itself with slanting stitches, as illustrated. This keeps the top part of the fabric completely vertical, and will help the gathers to hang completely straight when the stitching is finished.

Top-stitch through the folded band, to secure the gathers, then complete the waistband in the usual way. (Remove basting and trim away the extra gathered area inside the waistband first.) This method can be adapted for attaching perfect frills to a hem, by making several lines of basting, between the lines of a gathered frill, and one above the actual stitching line, so that the frill itself sits completely flat (FIG 7A, 7B, 7C, 7D).

FIG 8

FIG 9A

FIG 9C

FIG 9B

To attach frills to a dress, à la Saint Laurent

A detail from a Saint Laurent dress, dating 1964, is readily adaptable by other dressmakers. The design was for a shift-shaped evening dress, cut to midi length, and made from a bubbly textured, lacy black fabric. The dress was carefully constructed in two parts – a simple foundation sheath in silk with a plain folded deep hem at the bottom, and one frill over the top (FIG 8).

The top frill was made as part of a shorter overdress, and as such moved independently of the under-frill – perfect for a dance dress. Even more painstaking in the working of the design was the extra detailing of the frills themselves. The top frill was made with a deep, 3.75cm (1½in) turning underneath, which acted as a bouffant device, to keep the frill standing out. The second frill, attached to the petticoat, was made with a similar undersection, this time 7.5cm (3in) in depth, so that it would stand out even further, under the weight of the first frill. The hem edges of both frills were very simply turned back once and finished with a broad herringbone stitch. No separately-attached hem binding was thought necessary. The only inside edge that was very carefully finished was the edge of the neck facing, trimmed to no more than a scanty 0.5cm (½in) of black chiffon (FIG 9A, 9B, 9C).

This detail serves to show that the couturier always suits the level of finish to the task in hand – there is as much flexibility in his technique, as there is in the designing. The idea is great encouragement to the dressmaker with less skill!

A glamorous design by Valentino, 1983.

CHAPTER TWELVE

Few designers have any clues today about technique, the shape of an armhole, the perfect shoulder proportion without football padding, the exact balance of line and silhouette. I think Valentino is the perfect couturier because of his workmanship and technique. His unique touch is to plant fantasy on super high technique. I never look on Valentino as an Italian designer, but as an international one.

So speaks John Fairchild, publisher of the Bible of the American and international fashion industry, *Women's Wear Daily*. Valentino is one of the few Italian designers to have received recognition and approval from the worldly clientèle who would otherwise shop in Paris, and furthermore, from the establishment of the French couture industry. His work is not copiable in the way that Chanel suits were, nor is it evocative of a particular social mood, like the 'Space Age' fashions of Courrèges and Cardin. For instance, it was an extremely chic Valentino model – a lace turtleneck over a pleated cream skirt – that Jacqueline Kennedy chose for her wedding to Aristotle Onassis, in 1968. For Farah Dibah, ex-Queen of Persia, Valentino made hundreds of outfits – she would fly him out to Iran for her fittings. And it was a Valentino, a petal-collared coat, that she wore when she left Iran to go into exile. The story of the couturiers began with Worth, setting the style for the French court, and comes full circle, in the work of a man who has been labelled the 'Italian Jay Gatsby of alta moda'.

Valentino Garavani was born in Rome in 1933, to a family well endowed with money and taste. His mother, Teresa was a formidable woman who had grand aspirations for her children. Both Valentino and his sister grew up in an atmosphere where much was expected of them. He remembers that he was always a dreamer; in some ways the high standards of his family life turned him into a thoughtful isolated child. But while his family may have been demanding, they were also loyal. When Valentino announced his intention to become a couturier, he met little opposition, and his father Mauro was able to come up with sufficient funds

for him to open his own salon in Rome, when the time came. Valentino remembers clearly, and simply, the moment in 1950 when he knew what his future world would be:

> I was on vacation with my parents and bored in the mountains but sketching dresses every day. When I went back home to Voghese, I had made up my mind to leave for Paris and begin my fashion career.

It is evident, and remarkable, that Valentino never had any desire to do anything other than be a couturier. He went to Paris and worked for five years at the house of Jean Dessès. His years there gave him a good grounding in the world of the rich clientele who would form the basis of his own enterprise, and also provided him with the opportunity to learn about fabrics. Valentino soon graduated to sketching designs and his original work samples reveal the fascination with elegance and high style that has remained a signature of his own approach and style, along with a love of rich and ornate fabrics.

After Dessès, Valentino joined the house of Guy Laroche: here he had 'more freedom, and more sense of construction, which allowed me to do a bit of everything, be more daring than I ever was at Dessès'. While at Laroche, Valentino moonlighted by supplying sketches for the grand lady of fashion, the Vicomtesse de Ribes, who was launching a little enterprise through a fashion magazine designed for the younger market. His contact with her, and her life style, added further to his understanding of the kind of woman for whom he would eventually be designing clothes of his own. The description supplied by his own biographer of the typical Valentino woman is irresistibly extravagant:

> His heroines populate rooms where daisies are arranged in Sèvres vases given by husbands or lovers from sales at the great auction houses, where blond Deauville wicker chairs covered with old warm blanket throws are placed next to Louis XVI fire mantles and Georgian mirrors, where an exiled king may find himself seated next to Iman, that gazelle-like African model.

Strange as it may seem, history proves that this apparently ridiculous category of womanhood actually exists. All that aside, the work of Valentino deserves to be appreciated in spite of the inevitable furore that accompanies it.

On his return to Rome, Valentino was able to set up his own salon, with financial backing from his father. His first collection in 1960, did not receive great attention, but gradually he gathered momentum – helped not a little by his recognition in America. Eugenia Sheppard, and *Life* fashion reporter Sally Kirkland, doyenne of American fashion, were his chief supporters, writing about his work and bringing him into the public eye. Valentino had succeeded (admittedly not alone but alongside the work of French designers like Courrèges and Cardin) in finding a way to break with the dignified, formal female elegance of the fifties – the look promoted by Dior and Balenciaga. Valentino replaced the stiffness with a new, casual elegance, but the drama was still present. In comparison with his French counterparts, however, his clothes never lost a certain glamorous prettiness: they were never so cool and abstract in conception as Courrèges', for example. Valentino himself says, 'I am designing with one conception from head to toe in any collection. I take my ideas all the way … I do not design anything for people who wish to be anonymous, disappearing into the mainstream of things'. No wonder that with this philosophy the world's richest and most extrovert women were soon at his door.

One of his most successful collections came in 1968, with all-white outfits, mini-capes, incorporating hoods. Then in 1969, he created his own version of the current 'Op Art' obsession in fashion. Following his interest in taking a theme through a collection, he produced a series of gypsy-inspired dresses in the same year – but gypsies with the grandeur of Spanish infantas. In 1970 he produced a Hollywood 'vamp' collection, in 1972 dresses coloured with the palette of Matisse, to make Edwardian chiffons for dining; and a year later, Gustav Klimt designs, with close-coloured, swirling patterns. In spite of close attention to a particular thematic area for each collection, like any great designer, Valentino has a sense for a dramatic change in the making: he anticipated the desire to change the length of clothes from the mini to the midi in the 1970s, creating particularly attractive versions with geometric prints.

Valentino's energy for work is apparently legendary, as is his calm and assurance. His publicity director, Daniela Giardina has described him at the time of a collection: 'He should be the man with the most tension at that time, but he instils confidence in me by his sureness. His sureness of ideas, his sureness of his creativity and his empire'. More appealing (though equally admiring) is the description from his directrice, Jane Hsiang:

> His fantasy is conveyed with authority, through his politeness and sense of primacy without being a dictator. When working with him the power of his dream is conveyed through the power of his terribly trembling, poetic hands.

However partisan these views may be, there is no doubt that Valentino has an extraordinary creative energy. At the time of preparing a collection, he is perfectly capable of catching an idea and working up 50 variations on a theme, each one developed enough for execution as a model, within a morning.

Most of Valentino's designs are 'grand' (though in general this is true of all Italian fashion designs as opposed to the French) and he is the 'king of the grand evening dress' as John Fairchild has christened him. But his work is distinctive because the 'grand idea' also works when scaled down to something simpler. A complicated evening dress, with a balloon-shaped skirt, decorated with a lily motif – as luxurious a conception as could possibly be devised – is mirrored in a simple dark wool suit, with the same lily motif appliquéd (but padded out for extra effect) on the jacket front. The man who could slip bunches of artificial silk cabbage roses into the lining of the guipure lace sleeve on an Edwardian blouse (purely for the pleasure of the wearer) was also able to create (in 1968) an evening suit, based on a man's dinner jacket, in plain white wool, but enlivened by a stunningly simple brocade waistcoat (with matching jewelled brocade cuffs added to the coat). Extravagance, in other words, is not the essence of his designing. Valentino is not interested in 'fancy dress' exclusively:

> The exaggeration that has gone before in the sixties or earlier moments in the twentieth century looks wrong. A woman dressed as a Peruvian peasant and sitting in a Louis XVI or Napoleon III room is ridiculous. On the other hand, there is a woman who may buy an antique dress in the Flea Market in London, and she is also well dressed.

Certain elements run through most of Valentino's work, and are worth noting as design elements that can enliven the simplest wardrobe. The first is his fascination with flowers – and roses in particular. None of his collections move very far away from a decorative element that includes petals, leaves, or the silhouette of certain flower forms, such as lilies, tulips, roses:

> Flowers are a living thing even in the abstract form in silk or gazar. A floral print is the most romantic, calming vision. When I see a floral print, my eye rests with a tranquillity of peace upon the image of woman. Dresses with oversized roses or tulips are something bold and yet mysterious, it is an evocative symbol of life, the earth, civilization and the beauty of creation. Put a woman in an Op Art, bold geometric print and it becomes an aggressive, non-romantic statement.

Valentino added bunches of flowers, made in silk or chiffon, to the shoulder or waistline of a dress, with unerring eye for the exact point of emphasis. Often, the bunch is positioned *inside* or *under* a frill, so that it evokes that living quality, nestling into the shape of the shoulder or the curve of a waist. Similarly, with flounced and frilled dresses, he will use heavy lace, but place it inside layers of tulle or chiffon, so that the effect of the ruffle or flounce is richer, and texturally

Beautiful collars, ruffles, frills and sheen from Valentino – christened as 'the King of the grand evening dress' by John Fairchild, fashion publisher.

left *Valentino Garavani at work on designs – he has been known to produce 50 variations on a theme in one morning, at collection time. His background, working for Dessès and Laroche, enabled him to define his ideal woman: very rich, glamorous, romantic, super-sensitive to textures and luscious fabrics. Most Italian couturiers have a very classy sense of drama, but Valentino is supreme in his expression of it.*

more interesting. Decorations are incorporated into a dress so that they become part of the overall structure – no other contemporary couturier can use bows, for example, to better intrinsic effect than Valentino. In one design, red satin is tied across a sheath of a dress, forming a giant bow on one shoulder, the shape of the strapless bodice, and with a balancing bow on a black hip. (Red is one of his favourite colours, next to black and white; his love of the colour dates back to a trip to Barcelona, made when he was 17. He went to a corrida, and saw the well-dressed ladies, sporting various shades of the colour, like a mass of flowers, and the image has inspired variations on the theme ever since.)

To quote John Fairchild, 'When you strip a Valentino look down to the much desired minimal base – that is a coat, a suit, a jacket, a beautiful skirt – you have something pure and beautiful.' It is probably for this quality that Valentino is picked as one of the 'best five' in Japan, the other four being Sonia Rykiel (French RTW separates designer) and Norma Kamali (New York boutique designer and owner), besides homegrown entrants, Kansai Yamamoto and Hanae Mori (another specialist in sumptuous evening wear).

It would be erroneous to create the impression that Valentino merely designs elaborate evening clothes for the jet set. This is not the case: his daytime suits are models of simplicity, his coats luxuriously elegant but very basic in shape. He makes a ready-to-wear collection, which is shown in Paris every January (started in 1975) while the couture establishment is based in Rome. In 1982 he launched a children's range, *Les Enfants*, following the menswear line, *Valentino Uomo*, which began in 1972. There is even *Valentino Piu*, which produces fabrics, wallcoverings, ceramic designs too. (With the studied introduction of the 'V' motif in his collections as early as 1966, Valentino was well ahead of the 'logo' and image labelling that became such a craze in the decade that followed.)

In spite of his great success over the past 15 years, Valentino has the talent to see the need to change direction and continues to develop. He feels now that while his glamorous customers need to be serviced, he no longer needs to dress an 'Ideal woman', but rather to follow the freer dictates of his designing impulse: 'Now I am more interested in my own style, my own ideas. I must like the clothes, not just the ideal of the clothes as personified by one woman.' As the years pass, his work gains more credibility and respect among the establishment. Hebe Dorsey, writing in the *International Herald Tribune* in the autumn of 1982, for example, was able to say, 'There is a seriousness and a professionalism about this collection that has endeared Valentino to the difficult Paris pros . . .'

Valentino sets a standard of appeal, an open flattery in his clothes, which is irresistible: a severe, finely-tailored suit has a beautiful flower added to the lapel. His clothes are undeniably romantic but assured, and the most hardened non-dresser would have to admit their effect. In an age when fashion has little authority or single direction, his confidence guarantees his success.

left A 1982 design, when peplums were the shape of the moment – but interpreted boldly, with padding, topstitching, and set off by a beautifully big bow – a favourite decoration.

above Valentino's love of flowers for couture work is always present – he once filled the lace sleeves of a dress with artificial silk petals, purely for the pleasure of the wearer – sensual more than luxurious?

Valentino's luxurious evening dresses rely for their effect sometimes on the richness of the fabric, encrusted with sequins, paillettes, hand-worked embroidery, or woven with costly metallic threads. There is no doubt that rare and expensive fabrics, in unusual widths, distinguish couture clothes from others. But many of Valentino's most successful designs are mere slips of satin or crêpe, made special by the addition of a huge flower or bow, and by the careful working of the seams and even more particularly, hems. Some of Valentino's techniques can be applied to other kinds of dressy clothes, such as fine silk frocks, party dresses, disco outfits or lightweight summery muslins and organdies. This section includes several unusual ways with hems, used both by Valentino and other couturiers, followed by a special section on hand-made flowers, one of Valentino's favourite 'signature' details, so that you can add an elegantly Italian flourish to your more fanciful designs.

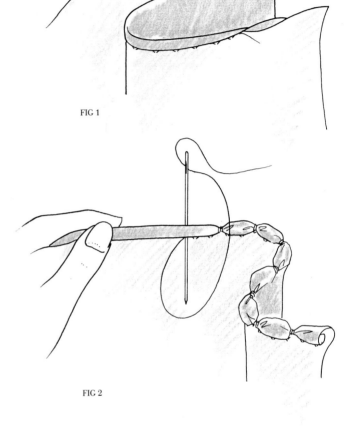

FIG 1

FIG 2

PART I – WORKING WITH FINE FABRICS

Here are a few hemming suggestions for use with fine fabrics, and some other more general notes on sewing with chiffons, silks, organdies, etc. First, these fabrics are difficult to work with accurately because they slip and slide about. The easiest way to minimize this difficulty is to layer each section of the fabrics with tissue paper: stitch the fabric sections, say for the bodice and sleeves, to pieces of tissue paper, one for each layer of fabric. Baste the tissue in place making sure that the selvedges remain straight at all times. Cut out the fine fabric *through* the tissue paper, so that no distortion of the pattern occurs.

Never mark a fine fabric with tailor's chalk or pins if you can help it. Use a very fine silk thread (not basting cotton) and a fine needle for making all sewing direction marks on the fabric. It often helps, when preparing seams for joining, to make two rows of small running as opposed to basting stitches, one close to the seamline, and the second slightly inside that, so that the fabric does not shift when

pushed through the sewing machine head. A good tip that follows for all basting and stitching work is consistently to use one direction of work – do not run up one sleeve and down the other; the slightest shift in the lie of the two sides of the fabric will be much more pronounced if the directions are reversed.

HAND-ROLLED HEMS

Couture clothes in fine fabrics nearly always have hand-finished hems, unless there are miles and miles of frills that merely require neatening off. The most frequently used finish is the hand-rolled hem, also the standard method for neatening the edges of scarves. The seam allowance is trimmed away to about a few millimetres (experiment with your own fabric, for the allowance left will depend very much on the weight of the textile) then simply roll the fine edge between finger and thumb to make a tight roll. Slip the fine needle and matching thread, holding the needle parallel with the edge, through barely two threads of the fabric, below, then make a second stitch in the fold. Do not draw the thread up too tightly, which will cause

puckering of the fabric. Work taking alternate stitches, above and below, keeping the roll taut in your other hand. The thickness must be even. The stitches should slip into the fold of the fabric and not be visible from either side (FIG 1).

SHELL HEM

An extremely pretty effect can be made on fine fabrics by taking the needle over the top of the roll at regular intervals, and making a second stitch over the first hem stitch, pulling tight so that you make regular 'shell'

shaped puckers along the edge of the fabric. This edging has a very thirties feel about it, well suited to satins and sheers (FIG 2).

ROULEAU INSERTION

This same stitch can be used to make a 'rouleau' insertion. Make a tube of fabric, a few millimetres wide, puckered by the stitching as just described. Fold a very narrow hem on both sides of the area to be insert-worked. Place a piece of tissue paper, underneath, and joining the hems exactly the

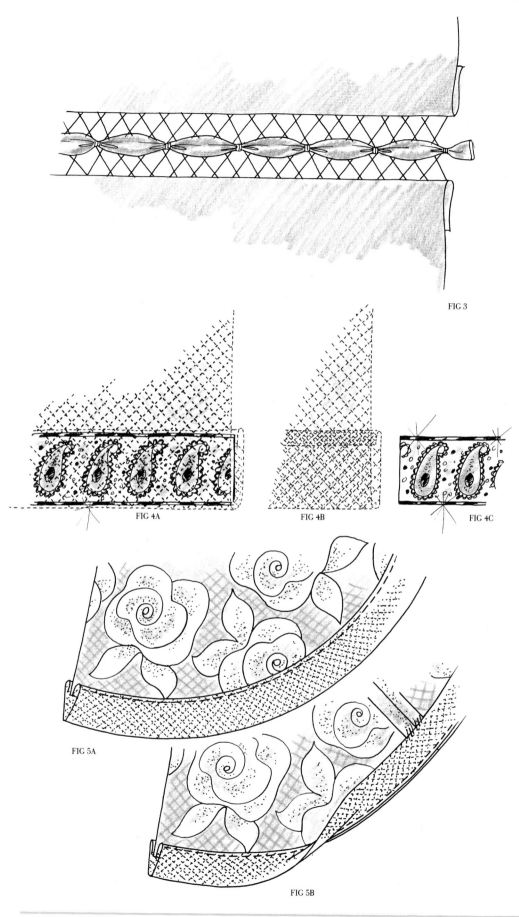

FIG 3

FIG 4A   FIG 4B   FIG 4C

FIG 5A

FIG 5B

required distance apart. Now tack the rouleau in place between these folded hems on to the paper. Work a suitable faggoting stitch between the hem edges and the shell-worked rouleau, as shown in the diagram (FIG 3).

BRAIDED HEM FINISH

A very simple but effective hem edging, found on a Worth black lace model dress, shows how to incorporate a rich gold or silver band into the hem of a lace or other sheer fabric design. This could look especially pretty on a full-skirted hem, or particularly elegant round the edge of a short jacket, with a matching silver or gold camisole-shaped top, beneath.

Measure the width of the gold or silver braid that will be inserted. Now fold up one narrow 1cm (½in) turning, then a second turning, exactly the width of the braid. Place the braid inside the hemfold created, but keep the first narrow turning to the back of the braid, so that it will not show from the right side. Either secure the hem by working with small running stitches, from the right side, or baste and then machine along the edge, very close to the top edge of the braid. (Hand work, of course, will produce a softer, prettier finish.) (FIG 4A, 4B, 4C)

GAUZE-BOUND HEM

Circular-cut lace skirts can be finished by folding a narrow length of gauze fabric, cut on the bias, and tucking this into a single turning of the lace or net at the hem. On Valentino's evening dresses this may be hand-finished, but sometimes very carefully machine-stitched close to the folded edge. The gauze helps the skirt edge to stand out attractively when complete (FIG 5A, 5B).

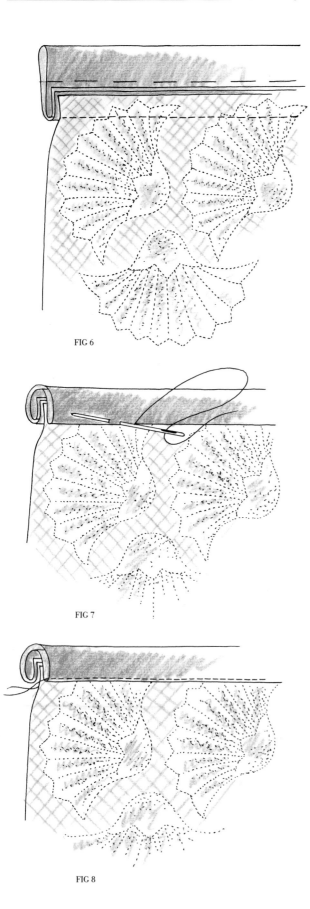

FIG 6

FIG 7

FIG 8

FRENCH BINDING HEM

This hem produces a bias-trimmed effect, but with a slightly thickened appearance. It is very useful for sheer fabrics, where you wish to make a neat edge, particularly on straight-cut edges, although the hand-sewing is very time-consuming. It uses up a considerable amount of self fabric, so bear this in mind if you wish to apply it to one of your designs: make sure to allow extra length on the purchase of the fabric in the first place.

Cut strips of fabric six times as wide as the required finished hem, on the bias of the fabric. Fold the fabric in half, with the right side facing out if there is one. Pin and then baste the two cut edges of the folded strip to the right side of the hem. Work all round the bottom edge, until within a few inches of the final join (**FIG 6**).

Open out the two ends of the strip, and make the join required on the straight grain of the fabric, judging it so that the circle will fit exactly to the skirt when folded back in place. (It is much easier to make this join by careful hand-sewing instead of resorting to the sewing machine at this stage.) (**FIG 7**)

Now machine stitch through the hem and the attached double bias exactly where the final depth of hem should be. Trim off any excess in the remaining depth of the hem allowance. Fold over the double bias strip to the wrong side. Baste, then slip-stitch along the basted line, over the top of the first row of stitches. When completed, the bias forms a rolled, opaque hem to sheer fabric . You can machine stitch this hem if you have yards to do (**FIG 8**).

PART II – MAKING FABRIC FLOWERS

One of the prettiest ways to make an outfit look distinctive, and to give it a Valentino look, is to add a flower or small corsage in the same fabric as the dress itself. This detail can lift an evening outfit out of the ordinary into a specially-created category, and add greatly to its glamour. The basics for flower-making are very simple, but the art does require practice in order to perfect it. The best way to proceed is to start making the flowers as close to nature as you can, simply for experience. More flamboyant gestures can come later, made by inventing fantasy flowers that suit the dress or neckline, in proportion and in luxury. Valentino uses flowers almost as a signature, frequently tucking them into or under the collar or frilled neckline of a dress, so that they add softness and luxury to a shape.

MATERIALS AND EQUIPMENT

The equipment required is simple, and readily available – glue, pins, boards and a selection of brushes. The fabrics you choose to use can vary greatly: lightweight satins, organdies, silks, are suitable for rose shapes. Thicker-petalled flowers such as pansies, tulips (or 'imagined' shapes) could well be made from velvet, corduroy, even tweeds or hessians. The secret lies in the application of a stiffening or 'sizing' agent – a water-soluble fabric glue. No fixed rules can be given about the amount or consistency of glue to apply: experiment on scraps of your chosen fabrics, watering down the glue, and painting it with a soft thick brush on to the back side of the fabric. (Pin the sample to a smooth flat surface such as a piece of sanded wood or a sealed cork tile, face downwards, for glueing.) You need to arrive at a finish that gives the fabric body without over-stiffness, so that you can stretch or crimp the shape, according to the petal effect desired.

Colouring agents are also required. For beginners, working on lightweight fabrics, permanent (i.e. petroleum-based) felt-tip marker pens offer the easiest method of petal colouring. In addition, a solvent such as rubbing alcohol, and small cotton wool pads are needed to rub over the felt-tip colouring, smudging and softening the shading naturalistically. Colouring can be removed by using a little bleach dissolved in water, and dabbing the area with soaked cotton-wool pads.

For larger-scale projects, fabric dyes, either in powder or in liquid form are available. The liquid fabric colours can be mixed in order to achieve subtle colouring effects.

You can use the dress fabric exactly in its own shade, or alternatively, create toning contrasts by using a white fabric, and dyeing a piece by hand to arrive at the colour desired. Try tie-dyeing for some pretty variegated effects. To colour petals, it is also very attractive to grade the colour, making it darker at the petal base, and paler at the outer edge (use bleach or alcohol as already described, to spread or fade the colour).

One important detail concerns the choice of glue – two types are suggested, a regular fabric glue for the basic mounting of petals, and a quick-drying glue for smaller details such as blossoms. Keep a needle and thread (matching)

for firming up the joins in the flowers too. Just as for florist's flowers, thin, thread-covered wire can be obtained from hobby or special craft shops, in various thicknesses: a thicker one, often found with green covering, suitable for the central stem, and a very fine type, used for stiffening individual petals or leaves sometimes. The flower stamens offer interesting design possibilities for the nimble-fingered. Ready-made types with small coloured heads or pearlized tops can be found, but the centres of flowers can be made from anything – pieces of broken jewellery, pearl buttons, loops of rich corded thread, dried and painted seeds – the material is endlessly variable.

Finally, remember that fabric flowers are delicate, and cannot be cleaned easily: freshen them with a coating of talc, lightly brushed off, followed by a steam over a kettle, and a gently remoulding, using the toothpick or knitting needle technique described later, if required.

TWO BASIC FLOWER SHAPES
Choose your fabic, and size it as already described. Dry quickly in a medium oven, or place on aluminium foil on a central heating radiator. Gently press on the right side to straighten out, using a dry cloth for protection. To make a fairly open flower shape, like a camellia, use the petal trace pattern given and cut out the number of petals required for the flower shape in mind. Follow the arrows for the direction of weave as the bias is essential for forming the shape of the petals. Cut some petals slightly smaller, to create an inner layer, making the flower more naturalistic. If desired, cut a calyx and a leaf or two from the patterns. (**FIG 9A, 9B, 9C**)

FIG 9A

FIG 9B

FIG 9C

Next assemble the stamens: use heavy corded silk twist and loop it several times through a small hook formed at one end of the stalk wire, as shown. Then, before mounting the petals, pull each one at the curved outer edge, stretching the bias, so that a rippling edge is formed. For a soft effect, the petals can be gathered round the stamen centrepiece, and lightly stitched at the base (FIG 10).

Alternatively, for a stiffer finish, where you wish to bend each petal outwards in a particular arrangement, use the fine size of wire, and place it between two petals, wrong sides facing, leaving enough 'stalk' sticking out so that you can twist this round the central stem. Glue the two sections of petal together, as shown. Mount these, one by one, smaller layer first, round the stalk, pinching and pleating each petal as you work. (On light fabrics such as gauze or lawn, a ridged effect can be achieved in each petal by scoring down the shape with a sharp pointed object on the right side, over a soft surface such as a felt pad, to produce a veined look.) (FIG 11)

The flower can be finished by poking a hole in the calyx piece, pushing this up the stalk, moulding it into place, and securing with a few stitches. Wind silk twist in buttonhole stitch down the length of stem required, or bind round it with silk ribbon, if preferred.

Small background flowers can be made by using the second trace pattern given, and looping one, then another, and then a third, through a hooked stem wire, as shown. These make a pretty addition to a small corsage (FIG 12).

LACE FLOWERS

More abstract and charming flowers can be made from old scraps of lace, or any narrow fabric with a scalloped or decorated edge. The principles are the same: the lace may be sized first for stiffening. Make a small centre piece, in place of a stamen, by using a jewelled button or a velvet-covered disc, stitched to a short piece of looped stem wire. Now gather up a strip of lace, about 25cm (10in) long, into a circle, as shown. Push this up the stem, and use a few small stitches, and a few dabs of fabric glue to secure the centre of the lace to the stamen-button. Several layers of lace, in graduating widths, could be added to this first layer, for a sumptuous effect. Try mixing layers of net between layers of lace, to help give the flower body, and to add texture or colour (FIG 13).

Leaves for backing could be cut from brocade or velvet, using the patterns shown, sized according to the stiffness desired, and then glued into double layers with a stiffening wire placed between the layers. Wind each leaf round the main stalk and add a few stitches to keep the leaf in position.

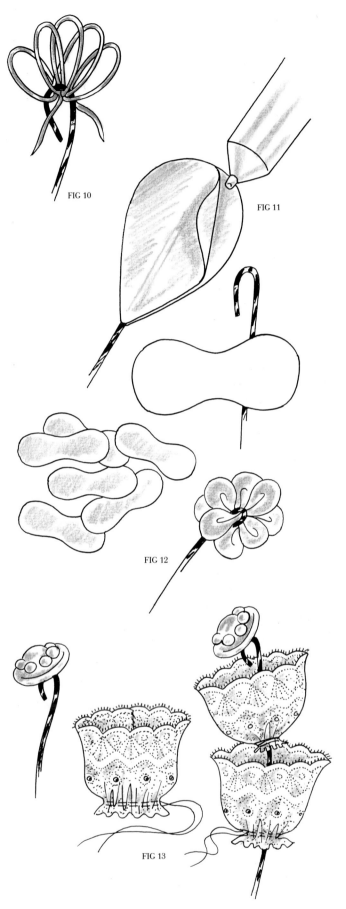

FIG 10

FIG 11

FIG 12

FIG 13

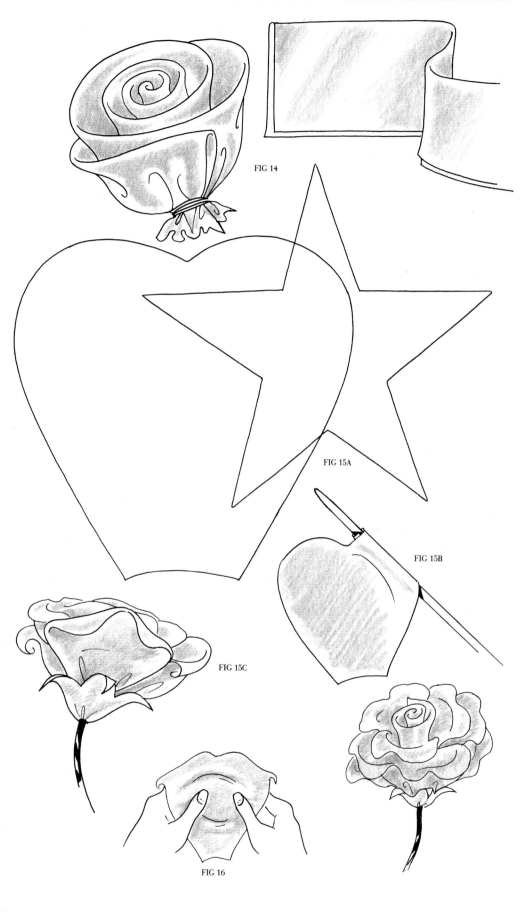

CABBAGE ROSE

The centre piece of a rose-type flower is easily made by folding a strip of the chosen fabric in two, on the bias. The piece needs to be at least 20cm (8in) long, and roughly 13cm (5in) wide. Start rolling the folded strip round a hooked stalk wire, by attaching one end with a few stitches, and rolling gently, with a slight spiral effect. (This basic 'bud' shape could be adapted to make interesting decorations in much thicker fabrics – Dior used to make big 'tweedy roses' along these lines.) Once the roll is completed, stitch the last edge to the layer just underneath, close to the stalk, to prevent it unrolling (**FIG 14**).

Now cut the petals using the diagram, and grading the sizes according to taste. If the rose is being made from organdie or silk, the edges of the petals can be rolled round a toothpick or even a fine knitting needle, to give the characteristic rose edge. Push the rolled area between the fingers, while on the stick or needle, and a realistic frilled edge results. Also, pull at the centre part of the petals, to give a rounded shape. The inner layer of petals should be mounted with the rolled edges curling inwards, then outwards for the bigger petals, as shown. If required, a calyx can be cut from the trace pattern supplied, and slipped up the central stalk in the usual manner (**FIG 15A, 15B, 15C**).

For other fine flowers, such as lily shapes, another trick is to dampen the sized edge of the petal with a thin layer of glue, and to roll it between finger and thumb (like the hem edging described on page 122). When the glue dries, an attractive rolled edge will remain (**FIG 16**).

FIG 14

FIG 15A

FIG 15B

FIG 15C

FIG 16

Look at a design, then adapt it to something you can make yourself. In Designers' Notebook you will find a host of ideas taken from the work of the couturiers in this book. They range from those that are purely decorative details, to others that require whole outfits to make them a practical reality. In most cases you can adapt your own existing patterns or alter readily available classic shapes. The appropriate couture technique is given in each case.

These two coat designs come from the Autumn 1958 collection of Pierre Cardin, and show all the drama that is conveyed by a strong silhouette and impeccable workmanship. For inspiration only!

right *Dramatize a jacket front by setting the button fastenings very close and cutting the jacket fronts a little wider than usual. Avoid bound buttonholes in a loose weave or soft fabric, as Balenciaga did in this Autumn 1964 design, originally in bouclé tweed. Use rouleau fastening, see page 86.*

right *Schiaparelli had buttons specially commissioned, like these pretty stars, Autumn 1937.* left *Develop an eye also for seeking an unusual effect, such as echoing fabric patterns, either with modern plastic buttons, or antique, often unusually-shaped ones. Add a good finish with bound button- holes – not too difficult on a firm light fabric, see page 51.*

Buttons

below *A simple Balenciaga wool coat, Spring 1968: hardly altered from the original which was made with a yoke to give shape, but with the stripes exactly matched. The off-beat element is the buttons, each one covered in a different colour fabric to match the stripe in which it is set. You could make your own covered ones or exploit mass button manufacture, mix-and-matching a set.*

A design that is as fresh now as when it was first shown by Schiaparelli, in Spring 1935, trimmed with a lavish care now seldom seen. Only five of the tiny handworked buttonholes are intended to fasten, the rest, with matching berry-buttons, are purely decorative. Handworked buttonholes, page 50.

below *Quicker to copy, but equally unusual! A Schiaparelli idea, from a Spring 1951 design – buttons in graduated sizes. (Originally used on a nipped-waisted suit, to echo the cut.)*

below *Dior used buttons to achieve a different effect here, Autumn 1958, not as pure decoration but to emphasize line. The idea is reinterpreted for trousers, right. If you cannot face the buttonholes, see page 50, consider decorative seaming, on page 94.*

left *Schiaparelli's use of early plastics was suitably innovative. Use a toggle as she did in Spring 1933 for a wool coat-dress. Hand-made rouleau, see page 86. Follow the detail with the cuffs too.*

left *In her original Spring 1933 design, the buttons were made of ivory and metal to trim a silk blouse. The square shoulders were achieved with stiffened canvas. Copy the idea in today's more unstructured line with wooden toggles.*

above *Cropped jackets can cross over with one simple fastening: Dior, Autumn 1961 – a jacket virtually unmodified in this sketch. Setting a collar, see page 71; rouleau, page 86.*

133

left *A design by Pierre Cardin, Autumn 1964, looking as sharp now as it did then. Adapt the tabs for a belt carrier and add flap pockets for an easy addition to gathered-top trousers. Patch pockets, page 88. Add decorative topstitching for emphasis, see page 94.*

near left *A couturier always pursues a trimming detail with a hint of exaggeration – but no arbitrary placings, as in this model closely based on a Dior, Autumn 1959.*

right *Pierre Cardin made some futuristic designs in white with navy trim for his Spring 1967 collection. modified here for a boxy top. Appliqué a trim to match a soft roll collar. For other decorative details see page 23 and page 41.*

Schiaparelli loved exotic trims – gold fringe, not entirely unrelated to the love of bold furnishing decoration for lampshades that existed at the time, was added to a fine black wool dress, Autumn 1936. Use the same approach on a more modern line. For ways to handle fine fabrics see page 122.

right *A Dior dress, Autumn 1958, shows the use of scale in achieving a decorative effect. The width and length of the bow complement the neckline perfectly. Never understate or underestimate a trimming; it is one advantage the dressmaker has over ready-to-wear.* below *The big bow is reinterpreted on a smock dress. For setting collars see page 71.*

left *An equally beautiful bow applied to one shoulder, based on a Cardin, Autumn 1965.*

More bows and trims:
below *Tuck a fabric flower* à la *Valentino behind a bow, see page 125.*

below right *Alter a simple smock top pattern to give pleats instead of gathers for this boxy jacket with a bow – another idea inspired by Dior's coat dress. Pleats, see page 112. To interface the collar, see page 70.*

below left *Alternatively, set off a plain faced round neck by mounting a chunky rolled and stuffed rouleau – taken from an Autumn 1958 Cardin coat design. This could be added to any simple batwing-sleeve top.*

left *This jumpsuit is not as difficult as it first looks: ruche the fabric top to fit a batwing sleeve pattern, as shown on page 23. Then add trousers with a seam below the waist. A long back zip allows entry. The ruching and the plaid pattern both come from a Poiret design, August 1926.*

above *Unusually decorated pleats, designed by Poiret in Autumn 1920. The fur inside the pleats is still a sensation. Pleats, page 112.*

left *A perfect way to use the applied folded trim described on page 25: one of Worth's favourite techniques and used by his house for a jacket exactly as sketched here in Spring 1925.*

above *An embroidery design taken from a Poiret dress with matching jacket in Autumn 1919. The entire waist area of the brown satin dress was embroidered with the design matched on the corners of the jacket. Linking decoration in this way is a successful idea to copy with machine or hand embroidery.*

right *A jacket design as shown by Poiret in Spring 1927, except that trousers have replaced the simple long skirt of the original. Like the bolero, the effect is made by repeating areas of decoration – especially pretty on the sleeves and trouser hems.*

left *A stunning pale wool coat by Courrèges, Autumn 1963, combines patch and welt pockets, see pages 88 and 52. Apply these to a modern, less bulky coat too.*

below *Balenciaga off-set the luxury of raw silk by using simple patch pockets on a front seam, Spring 1954. Adapt the basic idea by making a deep cuff with zips. For attaching a cuff – the same for a top as for a sleeve in principle – see page 79.*

above *Make tailored bulky wool look luxuriously casual, emulating a Balenciaga Autumn 1964 model. Dramatize the pockets by making them bigger than usual. Patch pockets, see page 88. Welt pockets, page 52.*

centre and above *The same shape can create an entirely different effect in different fabrics and colours. Welt pockets add a strong vertical emphasis to the side-fastened jacket, taken from a Cardin coat, Autumn 1965.*

right *A curving yoke was used by Balenciaga for a formal opera coat in heavy satin, Autumn 1957. The collar is cut on the bias which creates the soft roll and is interfaced for firmness. Collars, see page 71; interfacings, see page 68.*

below *A similar stiffened collar can be softened with an inner ruffle of ready-pleated lace or organza for a classic romantic look.*

above left *Seldom seen nowadays but an easy idea to adapt, are the asymmetrical revers, used by Saint Laurent in Spring 1968, in white piqué on wool. They could work equally well in leather, suede or suede fabric for a blouson jacket.*

centre and above *Two more Saint Laurent collars. Variations on Edwardian sailor-collared girl's dresses, shown in the Spring 1967 collection. Both are made more perfect by hand-stitching bound buttonholes, see page 50. For attaching cuffs see page 79.*

below *A beautiful suit shown by Cardin in spring 1971 (originally with a knee-length skirt). Adapt a classic suit pattern to make the scallops, as shown on page 102. For inserting a lining into a jacket, see page 58. Topstitching, see page 94.*

above right *One of the best maxi-coat designs, also by Cardin, Autumn 1970. The simply-constructed pockets are integrated into the design by the topstitching – apply this to pockets before handsewing to a garment.* right *Lightweight jersey could be given a similar treatment.*

below *The two scalloped dresses were suggested by a two-piece from Cardin, Autumn 1960, where the shapes were used to add surface interest to a simple design.* right *Attach gathers to a scalloped yoke. Gathers, see page 114; scallops, see page 102.*

left *A fabric can suggest a decorative detail: Chanel zigzagged a hem following a wavy-patterned fabric in Spring 1930.*

above *Couture hems are often padded to give a soft or thick rolled effect, and can emphasize fabric well. Stripes rolled in this way were shown on a Cardin coat, Autumn 1967. Padded hems, see page 105.*

right and below *The original Poiret dress was constructed so that the sleeves, neckline and waist tie were all formed from one scarf-like piece of fabric under a trousered pinafore, Spring 1928. Use an antique scarf or a yard or so of expensive sheer fabric to copy the idea, with a frilly peplum. Handling sheer fabrics, see page 122. Working the faggoting or pulled thread edging as in the original, see page 123.*

below right *Add these easy dropped frills to a simple summer dress. A Chanel design August 1933. For how to make a bias-cut frill, see page 42.*

left and right *Two variations on a Cardin design, Autumn 1966, emphasizing a wide armhole with topstitching, see page 94. This could be applied just as successfully to a pinafore dress.*

below *A swagger-back jacket, a Dior design in checked wool, Spring 1948. For the original, the whole jacket would have been canvas-backed to help it stand out well. Nowadays only the big wide cuffs and deep collar would need interfacing to hold their shape, see page 69.*

left _A fringed suede corselet like this was designed by Yves Saint Laurent for a dress and a short boxy jacket, Autumn 1967. It makes an eye-catching accessory for any outfit, hand-stitched and punched in soft suede._

right _For her Autumn 1934 collection, Schiaparelli demonstrated her love of incongruity by roping a silvered white lamé dress. Individualize a plain jacket, in the same way, with heavy cord, available in furnishing trimming departments, if not at haberdashery._

below *Claire McCardell liked to add ample accessories to simple clothes, like this very long obi-style sash for a shirt or dress, Autumn 1956. (But make it* long!*)*

right *Unusual belt carriers found on a Cardin dress, Autumn 1969 – make round, stiffened shapes, using the same lining method as for patch pockets, page 88.*

below *Dior made a simple day dress with a matching buttoned cummerbund, Autumn 1958, and echoed the fastening with buttons placed off-centre down the skirt. The idea is updated with this jumpsuit.*

Pleats

left *Pleats are classic, as you can see from the modified version of a Cardin model, Spring 1965. For the blouse, pleat up a fine, firm fabric, before cutting out a simple shape. Top or understitch to hold the pleats.*

below *A simple Yves Saint Laurent bowed inverted pleat, on a plain wool dress, suggested this pinafore. See page 113 for a useful way to finish inverted pleats.*

Three designs, hardly differing from their original conception:
left *Top-stitched pleats, Chanel, Spring 1972.*

centre *An asymmetric effect, with tucks in the bodice followed by pleats in the skirt, Dior, Spring 1973.*

right *Buttons for an inverted pleat, Saint Laurent, Spring 1965. Ways with pleats, see pages 112 to 114. (For the dresses, use a basic pattern but pleat up the fabric before pinning and cutting out.)*

151

below and right *Two designs inspired by a Dior coat, Autumn 1971, where the sleeves were lined with fur and left open, caught by ties. Adapt the effect by using fur trim caught in seams, or to line a coat-dress – both ideas could be applied to a number of simple pattern shapes.*

above *Schiaparelli used surreal notions that still seem daring: an Autumn 1935 model originally made in exclusive seal skin. Use a fur fabric.*

centre and right *Valentino uses flowers in many models, like this version of an evening dress, Autumn 1964, where the sleeves were covered with brocade flowers. How to make your own, see page 124.*

below *Pierre Cardin added a tweed rose for a tweed dress, in Autumn 1958 – a very simply-achieved decoration. To make a fabric rose, see page 127. (Other flower shapes are also shown.)*

Every fashion show concludes with a bride or party finale, so Designers' Notebook will make no exception. These designs owe their inspiration to Valentino, who made an evening dress with a candy-bow bodice, in red on black, shaped like the swimsuit sketch shown **below right.** *All these shapes have been decorated as described in the introduction.*

154

The couturiers like to work sometimes from the inspiration of the fabric alone – pinning and creating on a form. It may take many years to perfect a particular cut and look, but the essence of the art is conveyed in these easy sketches. For once, they require little sewing! It is hoped that these notebook pages will encourage you to let imagination wander and look more creatively at other designs, to make your own adaptations. Adding luxurious detail to basic shapes makes dressmaking more innovative and individual. The history of couture started with the works of Worth, pinning and stitching for a temporary effect. Like the couturiers, suit the level of craft and skill to the objective in mind.

Anatomy of Design 1 vol. Lectures published by the Royal College of Design, London 1951

Amies, Hardy *Just So Far* Collins, London 1954

Anthony, P and Arnold J *Costume: A General Bibliography* Costume Society, London 1974

Beaton, Cecil *The Glass of Fashion* Weidenfeld & Nicolson, London 1954

Bertin, Celia *Paris à la Mode* Harper & Row, New York 1957

Braun, Adolphe A *Figures, Faces, Folds* Batsford, London 1929

Brockman Helen L *The Theory of Fashion Design* John Wiley & Sons, New York 1965

Charles-Roux, Edmonde *Chanel and her World* Weidenfeld & Nicolson, London 1981

Crawford, Morris D C *Philosophy in Clothing* Brooklyn Institute of Arts and Science, New York 1940

Crawford, Morris D C *The Ways of of Fashion* Putnam, New York 1941

Davenport, Millia *The Book of Costume* 3 vols., Crown, New York 1948

De Graw, Imelda *25 Years/25 Couturiers* Denver Art Museum, Denver 1975

De Marly, Diana *The History of Haute Couture 1850–1950* Holmes & Meier, New York 1980

La Dépêche de la Couture 4 parts 1 vol., Paris 1952–3

Dior, Christian *Christian Dior's Little Dictionary of Fashion* Cassell, London 1954

Dior, Christian *Dior by Dior* tr. A Frazer, Weidenfeld & Nicolson, London 1957

Dior, Christian *Talking about Fashion* tr. Chavanne and Robourdain, Putnam, New York 1954

Garland, Madge *The Changing Form of Fashion* Praeger, New York 1970

Garland, Madge *The Indecisive Decade* Macdonald, London 1968

Gernsheim, Alison *Fashion and Reality 1840–1914* Faber & Faber, London 1963

Glynn, Prudence and Ginsburg, Madeleine *In Fashion: Dress in The Twentieth Century* Allen & Unwin, London 1978

Haedrich, Marcel *Coco Chanel Her Life, Her Secrets* Little Brown, Boston 1972

Hawes, Elizabeth *Why Is a Dress?* Viking, New York 1942

Hird, Anna L *Principles and Practice of Needlework* Anglo–Scottish Press 1943

Jakway, Bernard *Principles of Interior Decoration* Macmillan, New York 1922

Jarrow, Jeannette and Jondelle, Beatrice *Inside the Fashion Business* John Wiley & Sons, New York 1965

Keenan, Brigid *Dior in Vogue* Octopus, London 1981

Latour, Anny *Kings of Fashion* Weidenfeld & Nicolson, London 1958

Laver, James *Modesty in Dress* Heinemann, London 1945

Laver, James *Style in Costume* OUP, London 1949

Lumsden, Jean B *Stitches and Frills* Faber & Faber, London 1954

Lynam, Ruth, Ed. *Paris Fashion* Michael Joseph, London 1972

Mason, Gertrude *Tailoring for Women* A & C Black, London 1953

Mauck, Frances F *Modern Sewing Techniques* Macmillan, New York 1963

Morris F R and Wray E *Dress Design* Tailor & Cutter, London 1953

Morris F R *Ladies Garment Cutting* New Era, London 1950

Morton, Grace M *The Arts of Costume* John Wiley & Sons, New York 1964

Picken, Mary Brooks *Instruction Papers 1917–23* Scranton Pennsylvania WI Domestic Arts, Scranton 1923

Picken, Mary Brooks *The Language of Fashion* Mary Brooks Picken School, New York 1939

Poiret, Paul *My First Fifty Years* Gollancz, London 1931

Rathbone, Lucy and Tarpley, E *Fabrics and Dress* Houghton Mifflin, Boston 1943

Rochas, Marcel *Vingt-Cinq Ans d'Elégance à Paris* (published by author), Paris 1951.

Saunders, Edith *The Age of Worth* Longman, London 1954

Schiaparelli, Elsa *Shocking Life* JM Dent, London 1951

Squire, Geoffrey *Dress, Art and Society* Studio Vista, London 1974

Thaarup, Aage *Pinpoints* 2 parts, London 1939

Tomerlin Lee, Sarah, ed. *American Fashion* FIT/Quandrangle, New York 1975

Trois Fontaines, Jeanne *Dressmaking* Virtue & Co, London 1933

Vreeland, Diana *Inventive Paris Clothes 1909–1939* Thames & Hudson, London 1977

Whife A A *Art of Garment Making* Tailor & Cutter, London 1962

White, Palmer, *Paul Poiret* Studio Vista, London 1973

Woods, Pamela, *Flowers from Fabrics* David & Charles, Newton Abbot 1976

Worth: The House of Worth catalogue published by Brooklyn Museum, New York 1962

Worth, Jean P *A Century of Fashion* Little Brown, Boston 1928

Picture Credits

The Publishers would like to thank the following for the use of their photographs (t=top, b=bottom, l=left, r=right):

Art et la Mode 65 r; BBC Hulton Picture Library 10, 66, 108; BBC Hulton Picture Library/The Bettman Archive, Inc. 26; Cecil Beaton, Courtesy of Sotheby's, London 8, 38 tl, 48 l, 54; Pierre Cardin/Michel Boutfeu 98; Courrèges 90, 92 b; Courrèges/Jean-Philippe Decros 14, 92 t; Gazette du Bon Ton 28; International Wool Secretariat 11 b, 100 r; Maria Martel, USA 80, 82, 83, 84, 85; The National Magazine Company Limited/Harpers Bazaar 12 b, 74, 121; The National Magazine Company Limited/Harpers & Queen/Marc Hispard 120; L'Officiel de la Couture 12 t, 38 tr, 44, 47, 56, 57 b, 74 tl; Popperfoto 11 t, 46, 62, 100 l, 109; The Queen 18, 20 l, 30; Topham Picture Library 57 t, 110; Union Français des Arts du Costume 20 r, 31, 36, 38 b, 48 r; Union Français des Arts du Costume/International Wool Secretariat 111; Union Français des Arts du Costume/Marc Hispard 106; Union Français des Arts du Costume/P H Pottier 72; Union Français des Arts du Costume/L'Officiel de la Couture/P H Pottier 65 l, 75; Valentino/Horst 116; Valentino/Malinoweki 119 t; Valentino/Sposito 119 b.

The publishers would also like to thank Jean-Loup Charmet for his photographic work at UFAC in Paris.